Fresh Water Pearls

The Collected Poems of

Pearl Merriman Howerton

• *The Current River Poet* •

Compiled by **Bonnie Risby**

Acclaim Press
MORLEY, MISSOURI

Acclaim Press
— Your Next Great Book —

P.O. Box 238
Morley, MO 63767
(573) 472-9800
www.acclaimpress.com

Book & Cover Design: Frene Melton

Cover Photo: The Current River between Welch Spring, Missouri and Akers, Mississippi.
Photo by Kbh3rd courtesy Wikimedia Commons.

ISBN: 978-1-948901-25-3 | 1-948901-25-0
Library of Congress Control Number: 2019903247

First Printing: 2019
Printed in the United States of America
10 9 8 7 6 5 4 3 2 1

Contents

About the Collection

Often referred to as the Poet Laureate of Ripley County, the Current River Poet, Poet of the Ozarks, and Poetess of the Hills, Pearl Howerton spent most of her nearly nintey-five years living in and around Doniphan, Missouri.

Receiving little formal education, Pearl never studied couplets, sonnets or iambic pentameter. But she was a voracious reader steeped in the oral traditions and musical legacy of her forbearers. Inspired by the people, events and beauty around her, she hurdled deficits of schooling through her acquaintance to literature and songs.

Orlando Lewllyn Merriman, skillful in carpentry, helped to build churches wherever he settled his family. Merriman taught his children to sing and perform hymns using shaped notes. Pearl, his eldest daughter, committed multiple verses of hundreds of church standards to memory at an early age.

A faithful patron of the Doniphan Library, the poet read aloud to entertain her family during the Depression years before the advent of television. The family had favorite authors, which she revisited often.

Composing verses her entire life, Pearl was legally blind by the time she created the majority of her poems. Relying on visiting relatives and friends to transcribe dozens of stanzas stored in her memory bank, explains why there are often two or more versions of the same poem. I have tried to include the best versions in this collection. While she lived, many of her poems were published in the *Prospect News* and other regional magazines and journals. In these cases, I have provided the versions that went into print.

I wish to thank all of Pearl's friends and family that have aided in not only jotting down Grandma's poems but also in collecting and preserving her legacy.

Pearl Merriman Howerton

June 14, 1888 – April 30, 1982
Author

Pearl Howerton, ca. 1957

Mack Henry and Pearl Howerton returned to Ripley County in 1925 after a stint in Corning, Arkansas where Pearl helped run her brother Clyde's boarding house while Mack cut pearl buttons from mussel shells and tried his hand at cotton farming.

They married in 1919 following the great influenza pandemic. The hub of Pearl's family still resided in Ripley County. Setting up housekeeping at several sites around Doniphan, the couple worked hard during the drought and Depression years to support their growing family (Loren, 1928 and Patricia, 1930). They also had three children born at Corning: an infant son who died in 1921, Maxine (my mother) born in 1922 and Lynn born in 1924. Their children also included Pearl's daughters: Dorothy (Mrs. Arthur Keeny) born in 1907 and Geraldine Boyd (Mrs. William Duncan) born in 1914.

A skilled seamstress and interior decorator, Pearl, tailored clothing as well as upholstering furniture, creating draperies, rugs, and cushions. Operating boarding houses in both Corning and Doniphan, Pearl could take simple ingredients and create meals fit for a king.

Aside from a life-threatening bout with Rocky Mountain Spotted Fever, Pearl was robust and strong during an era when many suffered from malaria, diphtheria, and cholera. Spunk and stamina enabled her to nurse not only her children but also friends and neighbors. When her son Lynn had a finger nearly severed during an accident, Pearl expertly tended the wound, saving the digit. She helped deliver at least three of her grandchildren.

Although spending most of her life in Ripley County, Pearl was born in 1888 in Kansas shortly after her parents traveled by covered wagon to homestead a tract of land near what is presently Kingman City. After several years, the family returned to the Ozark hills that Pearl loved so dearly. More of her family's prairie adventures are included later.

Ain't Gonna Cry No More

by Pearl Howerton
for her great grandson, Jimmy Breidecker on his fourth birthday

When I was a little boy
  I cried at everything,
From the smallest scratch
  To a sweat bee's tiny sting.

I cried when I had to go to bed
— On the stroke of eight,
And sometimes in the morning
  When I had slept too late.

I cried when sister licked the bowl
  When Mommy made a cake,
And sometimes when I ate too much
  I cried with the bellyache.

One day my daddy said to me,
  "You are too big to cry.
For when you hide behind your tears,
  Fun is passing you by.

Life is not a long parade
  Marched to the beat of drums;
You'll find some bitter with the sweet,
  Just take it as it comes."

When I couldn't go out to play
  Because my throat was sore,
I thought I'd never learn to say,
  "I ain't gonna cry no more."

I was doing very well
  Till the day my puppy died;
I shut my eyes to hold the tears,
  But I heard them fall inside.

When my daddy came home that night
  I met him at the door,
And through the blinding tears, I said,
  "I ain't gonna cry no more."

April Brides

by Pearl Howerton
for her great granddaughter Martha Frances Holland (April 1970)

April brides like April flowers
Bloom in the garden of love.
Flowers are nourished by April showers
And brides by their husbands' love.

May this little April bride
Just starting the journey of life
Walk happily by her husband's side—
A true and loyal wife.

May her path be strewn with roses
Down through the passing years;
And may she never feel
The thorns of doubt and fear.

She is fair as an April dawn;
Her smile outshines the sun.
She spreads great joy where ere she goes
And is loved by everyone.

May the gods watch over her
And surround her with loyal friends.
And may she find the pot of gold
Down at the rainbow's end.

This is the wish of her grandmother
Who's writing this little rhyme.
May peace and joy be with her
Throughout the years of time.

Autumn in the Ozark Hills

by Pearl Howerton
(October 1968)

I wander through the Ozark hills
  When the trees are red and gold
Painted by a master's hand
  With colors gay and bold.

I view the glowing hues of gold,
  Of topaz, and of brown
That dot the sunny hilltops
  Like jewels in a crown.

When I wander in the woodland
  It gives my heart a thrill
To see the radiant beauty
  Of my native Ozark Hills.

I know the autumn leaves must go
  And become a leafy mold
To shelter violets in their beds
  From the winter's blast of cold.

The trees will stand so lone and bare
  In the winter's rain and sleet
Till the softly falling snowflakes
  Spread a blanket 'bout their feet.

I've seen many things of beauty
  That my heart with rapture fills
But nothing quite so lovely.
  As autumn in the Ozark Hills.

Beautiful Hands

by Pearl Howerton

I know a pair of beautiful hands
Rough and worn by the work of love,
Yet with touch as soft and gentle
As the soft wings of a dove.

These beautiful little helping hands
Always busy through the years—
Hands that have soothed many troubled brows
And dried ten million tears.

These beautiful little helping hands
Reaching out to all the world,
Spreading joy and peace and comfort
Like a magic mantle just unfurled.

These beautiful little helping hands
Although not soft and white
Toiling in the vineyard of the Lord
Surely precious in His sight.

These beautiful little helping hands:
Hands that will never grow old,
Always reaching out to those
Who need a hand to hold.

Poets write of many things:
Of snow-capped mountains and desert sands.
But none whom I've known will ever write
Of these beautiful little helping hands.

Beneath the Poppies

by Pearl Howerton
(March 1969)

I walked among the poppies
That grow in Flanders Field
And crushed the crimson blossoms
Beneath a careless heel.

I gazed in awe and wonder
On that field of flaming red
And on the snow-white crosses
In that city of the dead.

I stood in humble silence
And bowed my head to pray.
They are not dead but sleeping
I heard a small voice say.

They sleep beneath the poppies,
These men in Flanders Field
And when we trample on the dust
I'm sure they somehow feel.

We are the guardians of this field;
We sprang from their bloodstained dust.
We raise our scarlet banners
In memory of their hope and trust.

We are a part of every man;
We sleep beneath this sod;
We lads who bravely gave our lives
For our country and our God.

Beside the River

by Pearl Howerton

Let me live beside the river
  And dream in the noonday sun,
Where men have lived, dreamed, and died
  Since Life and Time were begun.

Let me live beside the river
  That flows to distant lands,
And hope someday to gather my dreams
  From the white drifting sands.

Let me live beside the river
  Never weary nor forlorn,
Knowing that God in his wisdom
  Ever watches over his own.

Let me live beside the river
  Where all nature rushes by,
And listen to the music of the waves
  As they sing a lullaby.

Let me live beside the river
  And count my million stars,
Not dream of streets and cities
  That seem like prison bars.

I would be free as the raindrops
  That fall on the river's crest—
Marching like soldiers on parade
  Till it lays them down to rest.

Let me sleep beside the river
  Beneath my bit of sky,
With the forest and hills about me
  And my river flowing by.

Big Chief Clint

by Pearl Howerton
for her great grandson, Clint Brock (June 1972)

Listen my children and you shall hear,
The story of Big Chief Clint
Who shot an arrow into the air
And never found where it went.

Chief Clint is heap big hunter
Who roams the prairies wide,
With his trusty bow and arrow
And his tomahawk by his side.

He wear a chieftain's headdress
On his small dark head,
And always wants it near him
When he climbs into his bed.

Big Chief Clint has a sister,
He calls her little Desert Flower
They often dance the rain dance
Around the bright campfire.

The paleface give him heap much trouble
Trying to take his hunting ground;
He chases them so far away
They never can be found.

If his paleface mother scolds him
When he has been bad
He stomps his feet and loudly yells,
Big Chief Clint am heap big mad.

When the long hard day is over
And he's ready for his bed
He's not a big chief anymore,
Just Mommy's little sleepyhead.

Bits of Truth

by Pearl Howerton

We come into this world with nothing.
Some acquire great wealth and fame.
But when the master calls us
We leave it as we came.

This world has many kinds of people:
The rich, the poor, the halt, the lame.
But a plot of earth six by three
Makes us all the same.

If we could see as far into the future
As we can when looking back,
I'm sure our speeding train of life
Would never leave the track.

If we could see ourselves as other see us,
Our pride might take a fall.
For the image we build up around ourselves
Others may not see at all.

He who helps a fallen brother
With helpful deeds and friendly smiles
Will find his pathway is much better
When he comes to the last, long mile.

Bobbling Brook

by Pearl Howerton
for her great granddaughter, Shelley

"Stop pretty water," said Shelley one day
To the frolicsome brook that was running away.
"You run off so fast; I wish you would stay.
My boat and my flowers you will carry away."

"But I will run after you; Mother said that I may.
Then I'll know where you're running away."
So Shelley ran on, but I've heard say
She never did find where the brook ran away.

Bonnie

by Pearl Howerton
for her granddaughter, Bonnie Lou Gibson on her nineteenth birthday

Poets write of famous men
Or ladies young and fair,
I would write of a lovely maid
With stardust in her hair.

She's like the sun at early dawn
She is always kind and sweet;
The laddies come from far and near
To worship at her feet.

She is always gay and happy
And loved quite well by all;
The lads that follow in her train
Come at her beck and call.

Although she's kind to one and all
She's really not a flirt
She lets them follow in her train
For she cannot see them hurt.

Although she smiles upon them all
She gives her heart to none
Who come to worship at her shrine
This goddess of the dawn.

This lovely maid is dear to me
As everyone can see.
May joy and gladness be her lot
Wherever she may be.

This tale is getting out of hand
And perhaps a little wild,
This gentle maid of whom I write
Is my very dear grandchild.

The Brooklet

by Pearl Howerton

I was once a little brooklet,
Flowing bright and free,
Singing a song as I moved along
  On my way to sea.

I sang to the flowers and grasses
  Along my sunny shore,
And to happy children
  Beside their cabin door.

I sang to God's small creatures
  That in the noontime heat
Came to drink my cooling waters,
  That trickled at their feet.

I flowed beneath the willow
  Where the silver crappie sleep,
And through the tall green rushes
  Where the lazy bullfrogs leap.

I raced beside the meadows
  Where barefoot boys at play
Wade in my icy waters
  At the end of a summer day.

I rambled through the woodland
  Where no man's feet have trod,
Beside the lofty mountains
  That seem to talk with God.

I flowed by hills and mountain
  streams
  That feed my hungry tide,
Till I became a river,
  Flowing deep and wide.

A rushing, roaring river
  Flowing wild and free
Carrying boats and cargo
  To the distant sea.

I, who was a brooklet,
  Singing, o' so free,
Will be lost and soon forgotten,
  In the mighty sea.

Carol

by Pearl Howerton
for her granddaughter, Carol Howerton

Beneath the lofty mountain peaks
Lives a little maid so fair;
Her eyes are dark as midnight
And auburn is her hair.

She's one with God and nature
Surrounded by her hills,
That seem to bow their heads in prayer
When everything is still.

She is always gay and happy
This little maid I know.
And in the bright warm sunshine
You can almost see her grow.

She plays beside the bubbling brook,
Wades in the water cool,
And talks to the pussy willows
On her way to school.

She visits with the fairy folk
Down in the shady nook,
And tells them of the stories
In her storybook.

She's always sweet and happy
This little maid so fair,
With joy and laughter in her eyes
And stardust in her hair.

May she never lose her faith and trust
Nor the laughter from her eyes.
And may her guiding star forever shine
Away up in the skies.

The Castle

by Pearl Howerton

I have a little son,
Who is very dear to me.
He brings me grief, as well as joy,
He's very small you see.

He plays beneath the table,
And climbs upon the chairs.
He built a Roman castle
Upon the cellar stairs.

I did not see this castle,
Though it was very tall.
At least, it seemed that way
To a boy, so very small.

So I tripped and down I fell
Right to cellar floor,
And the ruins that lay about me,
Were not a castle anymore.

I'm black and blue; I'm bruised and sore;
No bones are broken, I think.
But my baby's castle's ruined
Down to the smallest plank.

Take heed, my son, and all small fry,
Who have this building flare.
Trouble's bound to come between,
Your castles and the stairs.

A Cherished Friend

by Pearl Howerton

I have a cherished friend,
Of whom I think each day.
My thoughts take wing and visit her,
Though she's many miles away.

She makes me welcome in her home
When I chance to pass that way.
And when my skies are overcast
Her smile chases the clouds away.

Friends may come and friends may go
But few will come to stay,
Who with their loving kindness
Can turn your night to day.

True friendship is not measured
By the yardstick of success,
But by gentle words and kindness
To a friend in deep distress.

A true friend should be cherished
In this world of greed and strife.
They are like a shining beacon
On the troubled sea of life.

The Cherry Tree

by Pearl Howerton

George Washington had a little
  brother
Whose name they say was Ike,
Not so wise and bold as George,
But just a common tyke.

They romped and played together,
As little brothers should,
George had a little hatchet,
With which to chop the wood.

One day while playing in the field
They spied this cherry tree,
With the cherries shining red:
A pretty sight to see.

They could not reach the cherries
That was plain to see.
So little Georgie boldly said,
I'll chop down the tree.

Their father found his favorite tree,
Prone upon the ground,
With the cherries ripe and red,
Lying all around.

He yelled, he stamped, he madly swore;
An angry man was he.
Then he loudly shouted,
"Who cut down my cherry tree?"

Little Georgie shook with fear,
He knew he was bound to catch it;
So he boldly answered,
"Ike did it, Father, with my little
  hatchet."

His father being somewhat deaf
And likewise dim of eye,
Truly thought his George had answered,
"Father, it was I."

Oh, my son, my little son,
To me you could not lie;
Those words I will remember
Until the day I die.

It's all set down in history books,
For everyone to see,
But I would really like to know,
Just who chopped down that tree.

Christmas

by Pearl Howerton

Christmas Eve will soon be here
And the joys that it will bring,
Children all over the world will listen
To hear the sleigh bells ring.

Santa with his sleigh piled high
And the reindeer ready to go,
Will glide away in the silent night
Through the white and drifting snow.

Over the distant hills and mountains
With his white beard flowing wild,
He must hasten to bring
A Christmas gift to every child.

Santa knows no creed nor color,
Be they black or white,
Every child in all the world
Must have a Christmas gift tonight.

On Christmas morning there will be
Many gifts for everyone,
Don't forget the gift God gave us
The gift of His only Son.

Christy

by Pearl Howerton
for her great granddaughter, Christy Brock Whittymore (June 1972)

One bright and happy Christmas Day
A treasure came to me,
More precious than all the gifts
Beneath our Christmas tree.

This treasure was a baby girl
Sent from heaven above
To fill our home with sunshine
And to fill our hearts with love.

We call this treasure, Christy,
For the birthday of our Lord.
Her laugh is like an angels' choir
All singing in sweet accord.

She is like a golden sunbeam
Dancing everywhere:
Beneath the table, on the chairs,
And sliding down the stairs.

Sometimes she is an angel
With laughter in her eyes,
And sometimes a little imp
That fills us with surprise.

Imp or angel, good or bad,
We love this little sprite,
Who truly is an angel
When she says her prayers at night.

We thank you God for this small treasure
You placed within our care;
And may we ever be found worthy
Her precious life to share.

Cider Makin' Time

by Pearl Howerton

When it's cider makin' time at our house
Way down in the Ozark Hills,
My daddy always lets me help
Around the cider mill.
He lets me drive old Robin
When he goes too slow.
Melted around and around,
The juice begins to flow.

People come from far and near
With their jugs to fill
When it's cider makin' time at our house
Down in the Ozark Hills.
Sometimes the fellers bring their gals;
It really is a treat
To watch them drinking through a straw
That cider cool and sweet.

But when that cider stands a while
It sure ain't sweet no more.
And when I'd drunk a glass or two
I could hardly find the door.
I asked my dad why this was so;
He only shook his head.
You'll learn that secret all too soon
Is all my daddy said.

There's another thing that puzzles me
I guess it always will.
Where do all the little worms go
In that cider mill?
No one thinks of these small creatures
As they drink their fill.
But everybody's happy at our house
When it's cider makin' time in the hills.

Country Roads

by Pearl Howerton

Country roads take me home
Back down the years of time
To the hills where I was born,
To that childhood home of mine.

Country roads take me home;
Let me walk down memory lane,
Hear the coo of doves are early dawn
And robins singing in the rain.

Let me walk down country roads
As I did so long ago,
By the rippling streams and meadows
Where wild blue bonnets grow.

Let me wander through the valley
Down by the garden wall
With the scent of lilacs on the air,
When the evening shadows fall.

Country roads that ever wander,
Through the hills and by the streams,
To this weary heart of mine
Childhood years seem but a dream.

Let me see again familiar places
Where I always loved to roam,
When the dew was on the meadows.
Country roads please take me home.

The Covered Wagon

by Pearl Howerton
(January 19, 1968)

Of all the tales my grandpa told,
About the wild and woolly West,
The story of the covered wagon,
Is the one that I like best.

From the strong and pliable hickory
They made the wagon tongue,
Also the whiffle-trees and bows,
From which the canvas hung.

The axles and rocking bolsters,
Were made of seasoned oak.
Also the hubs and felloes,
And the short and sturdy spokes.

The wagon bed and over-jet
Were made of lightest pine
For it must hold a man's possessions,
Going west in forty-nine.

The bows were set securely,
And the canvas round them hung.
A welcome shelter from the rain,
And the boiling noonday sun.

My grandpa joined this wagon train
When he was very young.
He gambled all that he possessed
To follow the westward sun.

The covered wagon was his home.
And all that he loved best.
Was sheltered under canvas and bow,
As it rolled on to the West.

The wagon master ruled the train,
With a firm but kindly hand.
To each, a friend and counselor,
The leader of the band.

He sometimes read the burial rites
For one who passed away,
And was left beside the lonely trail,
To await the judgment day.

The covered wagons did not stop
For sorrow, grief, or pain,
The sturdy wheels kept rolling
Through swollen streams and rain.

For covered wagons were rolling west
Where land was for the taking,
Where tender heels were out of place,
And men were in the making.

The early West was never won
By gambling men and darts
But by the covered wagons
And men with fighting hearts.

That is what my grandpa said.
And he should surely know,
For he drove a covered wagon west,
In that time so long ago.

The Dahlia Lady

by Pearl Howerton

This gracious dahlia lady
Let me walk in her garden one day,
And shared with me the beauty
Of her dahlias in their bright array.

With the help of God and nature
And a pair of willing hands,
She created this lovely garden
In the midst of which I stand.

She truly has a green thumb;
Also a golden one;
And fingers that mold the soft damp earth
From which her dahlias sprung.

The colors of the rainbow
Had surely fallen from the sky
And touched each tiny petal
With gold and crimson dye.

This pink caught the color of the moon
With dew still on its face;
The tender beauty planted there
Nothing can e'er replace.

Still another caught the purple shadows
When the evening twilight fell;
Violet, lavender and heliotrope,
Colors we all know so well.

There is this tender white
Soft as a bridal gown;
With dew drops on its petals
Like diamonds in a crown.

Aahh! If I could only write,
What a story I could tell
Of this gracious dahlia lady
And the garden she loves so well.

Dancing Leaves

by Pearl Howerton

See the beautiful, dancing, autumn leaves
As they gaily skip in the morning breeze.
Miss Golden Maple, Mr. Elm so tall;
Dance the minuet on the garden wall.

Shy little Red Bud and Sycamore
Merrily skip from door to door,
Joining their happy little friends,
Who dance to the music of the winds.

The soft winds whisper, "Come my friends,
Come dance to the music of the wind.
We'll dance the schottische and Virginia Reel,
The light fantastic, toe and heel.

I'll swing you high; I'll swing you low,
As over the field and meadow we go,
Gathering friends along the way,
To join in the fun, this golden day.

Then folding my arms, I'll lay you down,
To sleep forever, upon the ground.
And happy children will remember the day,
When you so merrily danced away."

Dear Little Alice

by Pearl Howerton
for her granddaughter Alice Duncan Fisher (1954)

Dear little Alice, I think it's time
To write you another little rhyme.

I hope you are well and happy too
Doing the things you are told to do.

Helping Mother and going to school
And trying to learn the Golden Rule.

Don't pull the hair of any child
For it simply makes them wild.

And, Little Alice in Wonderland,
In the corner my have to stand. (again)

Little Alice of Storybook fame,
A little girl with a magic name,

Who crept through a keyhole one sunny
  day
Into Wonderland, so I've heard say.

All the birds and beasts were there;
The shaggy lion and the Cinnamon bear.

"Why call him Cinnamon?" sly Alice said,
"Why not chocolate (bar) bear, instead.

The big old lion said, "I do declare,
A little girl with golden hair,

"We must welcome her to Wonderland.
And this I'll have you understand,

Put on your very best manners and looks,
Just as they do in story books.

So our little friend will not take fright
And steal away in the silent night."

The big bull frog, on his lily pad
Said, "Well, by golly, I'm so glad

To see a child in our land of wonder
I think I'll croak. I will, by thunder!"

So he hopped and croaked and stood on
  his head
Till the wise old owl, very gruffly said,
"I think Mr. Frog should go to bed."

So Alice wandered in Wonderland.
But to this day I don't understand.

How Alice got home that wonderful
  night
Without giving her folks a terrible fright

When she crept through the keyhole of
  the bedroom door
And fell, kerflop, right onto the floor.

All you children who care to look
In the pages of this little book

Will find the magic Alice found that day
In Wonderland so far away.

So I will close as I've run out of time;
Hope you enjoyed this little rhyme.

Dedicated to Lou, A Very Special Friend

by Pearl Howerton

I have a very special friend
Who often visits in my home.
Her presence seems to linger
Even after she has gone.

She is a sweet and gracious lady
Who always wears a sunny smile.
Just to know she is my friend
Makes my life worthwhile.

To know her is to love her—
My friend so very rare.
She has love for everyone
And always some to spare.

As she travels life's long highway
Always sunny and sublime,
And in passing she will leave
Footprints on the sands of time.

Footprints that lead to many places
Where love and comfort she has shown,
Teaching many troubled souls
That they need not walk alone.

When her sojourn here is over
God will pilot her above
To that home he has prepared
And furnished with his love.

There to dwell eternally
With God upon his throne
And to walk the golden streets
In that heavenly home.

Perhaps, He'll have some work for her
In that home so bright and fair—
Helping some belated soul
Or dusting off the golden stair.

Thank you, God, for this friend.
May her life forever shine;
And may I ever be found worthy
To call her friendship mine.

Dedicated to the Nurses and Those Who Make My Life So Pleasant Here

by Pearl Howerton

I live in a lovely home:
A haven of rest for the weary.
The lightning may flash and the loud thunder roll
Yet my home is always bright and cheery.

I am surrounded with angels of mercy
Though they do not wear a halo.
But their friendly, smiling faces
Seem to wear a special glow.

They come in answer to my call,
Be it morning, noon, or night.
And whatsoever may be wrong,
They always make it right.

They do not seem to care
That I am old and gray,
But treat me very special
In their very special way.

Thank you, God for these friends
Who do so much for me.
And shower your blessings on them
From here to eternity.

And when my sojourn here is over
And I no longer see their smile
Let them hold my hand, dear Lord
And walk with me down that last, long mile.

Dedicated to Sheri, A Dear Little Friend

by Pearl Howerton
(May 19, 1975)

I have a lovely little friend
Who is very kind and sweet.
She is like a golden sunbeam
From her head down to her feet.

Like a lovely summer breeze,
She comes into my home
Bringing joy and sunshine
To me who lives alone.

To know her is to love her,
This little maid so fair,
With eyes that sparkle like the dew,
And stardust in her hair.

She does not seem to mind
That I am old and gray
But treats me very special
In her very special way.

She is very kind and understanding
Though our generation gap is very wide.
But my spunky little friend
Comes right over to my side.

There we make a happy merger
Into the world where dreams are made,
Where we spend many happy hours
Early spring and autumn shade.

We have many things in common
Though she is young and I am old.
My hair has turned to silver
And hers is purest gold.

May the gracious God watch over her
This little friend of mine
And shower His blessings on her
Right down to the end of time.

Dogwood Legend

by Pearl Howerton

This beautiful legend was handed down
From the time of Galilee,
When the Savior died upon the cross
Made from the dogwood tree.

This tree was chosen for its strength
For it was straight and tall,
The monarch of the mountainside
Towering over all.

This proud tree felt great sorrow
Bowed down with grief and shame
That it had thus been chosen
The Savior to defame.

The gentle Christ looked with pity
On this proud and sorrowing tree,
And promised henceforth and forever,
Small and twisted it shall be,

That never again would its strength be used
As a gibbet of suffering and shame.
It would bloom in radiant beauty
This promise to proclaim.

In the springtime it shall wear
A robe of blossoms white
In memory of the pain He bore
That man might see the light.

The four-petaled blossoms form the cross
On which the Savior died,
The rust brown tips are nail prints
That pierced His bleeding side,

The pale green centers flecked with red
The crown of thorn placed upon His head,
The berries that form when the petals fall
Like crimson blood drops shed for all.

This legend will live forever
And its beauty each spring we'll see.
A reminder that Jesus died on the cross
Made from the beautiful dogwood tree.

This legend has been handed down
Almost two thousand years,
When Mary knelt beneath the cross
And for her Son wept bitter tears.

Dogwood Time

by Pearl Howerton

God spread His beauty over the world
Like a magic carpet just unfurled,
He gave us rivers, lakes and rills
And dogwood in the Ozark hills.

Snow-white blossoms, crowned with green
Cast lacy shadows on the nearby streams.
The beauty is free, come drink your fill
When it's dogwood time in the Ozark hills.

When the dogwood blooms in the Ozarks
And the birds are on the wing,
The wild geese call and the mocking bird trills,
When it's dogwood time in the Ozark hills.

*As the red bud's beauty begins to fade***
And gone is the winter's chill,
No other season is quite so fair
As dogwood time in the Ozark hills.

The dogwood glows in pale moonlight
When the night is calm and still,
Their beauty is beyond compare
When they bloom in the Ozark hills.

California has the beautiful redwood;
With pine the northland is filled,
But we have the graceful dogwood
That blooms in the Ozark hills.

** *(I'm sure the first line of stanza four is missing. But it was printed this way in the* Prospect News *and I could find no other copy. I inserted a line that Pearl might have written.)*

The Door Mat

by Pearl Howerton

I'm just a lowly door mat
As everyone can see.
I answer every beck and call;
Just wipe your feet on me.

I'm just a lowly door mat;
I'm old beyond my years.
My eyes have lost their luster
From the flow of many tears.

I was once a person—
Happy, young, and gay.
Somewhere in this game of life
I got lost along the way.

I got pushed into a rut
And I lacked the will to rise.
While the world and all its beauty
Slowly passed before my eyes.

I'm just a trampled pussycat
Who lost seven of her lives.
I'll fight; I'll bite, scratch and howl
To keep the other two alive.

Sometimes I think I will rebel;
I'll rise right up and shout,
"I'm not a door mat any more
So everyone watch out!"

I'll paint my lips and curl my hair
And buy some pretty clothes.
I'll strut and swagger down the street
And see some picture shows.

I'll maybe take me out to dine
And drink a glass of gin.
I truly hope the sudden change
Don't do the ol' gal in.

Ah! This is but a wistful dream
And time is passing by.
I must hurry to the kitchen
And make a pumpkin pie.

Jack and Sue will be here soon
With little Tom and Kit.
They are going to see a picture show
And I will baby-sit.

But somehow, I do not mind
They are so very sweet.
So I'll just remain a door mat
With my babies round my feet.

The Dreamer

by Pearl Howerton
for her grandson, Randy Gibson (December 1972)

My grandson is a dreamer;
He dreams his way through life.
Sometimes at the dinner table
He spears vegetables with his knife.

His eyes are on the television.
His mind is far away,
Roaming in strange and distant places
That he might see some day.

He dreams along the woodland path
On his way to school.
Sometimes he is very late
Often breaking the teacher's rule.

She greets him with an icy frown
Saying, "Randy, you're late again!"
He melts the frown right off her face
With his wide and dreamy grin.

He dreams about the car he'll build
When he becomes a man.
He will enter her in races—
The swiftest car that ever ran.

He will soar on silver wings
Across the bright blue sky;
Maybe visit the Man in the Moon
And count the stars as they rush by.

Just a few more years to dream
And then he'll meet his fate.
He'll never know what happened
Until it is too late.

He'll meet a girl with golden hair
And a smile so warm and sweet.
If he can win her for his own,
His life will be complete.

Never lose your dreams, my son.
Shut the door and lock them in.
The storms of life may toss you about
And you may need your dreams again.

The dreamer holds a magic key
To the world where dreams are made.
He may enter as he will
To find the dreams that he's mislaid.

Everything Happens to Me

by Pearl Howerton

When I was just a little boy
Everything happened to me:
Mama took my bottle from me
When I was hardly three.

Of course, this broke my little heart
And stunted my early years.
I could not eat or sleep
And I cried an ocean of tears.

My daddy gave me a little dog
That sometimes slept with me.
One night I forgot to put him out
And that was a catastrophe.

My mother used her hairbrush
On a place I could not see.
I ate standing for a week.
Well everything happened to me.

When I was only six years old,
Disaster struck again.
My loose teeth started falling out
Leaving ugly gaps where they had been.

I'll never grow to be a man.
That is plain to see.
How could misfortune treat me so?
Well everything happens to me.

The Famous Watergate

by Pearl Howerton
(June 1973)

I'm just a plain dirt farmer
And have been all my days.
I don't know much about polly-ticks
Or them fancy, city ways.

But I do know about watergates
And how I used them on my farm,
To keep my neighbors' cows
From eatin' up my korn.

They say that up in Washington
They put one in a house
That folks had filled up with bugs
To force them Demmy-Krats out.

I do declare it is a sight
What folks will do through hate
Now they have our President
Plum astraddle of that Watergate.

I know he must feel bad,
Folks seein' him in that awful plite,
Just sittin' tite and hopin'
That things will come out rite.

The Father of Our Country

by Pearl Howerton

Men have done great deeds,
And bards have sung them well.
Now of brave George Washington,
I, a tale, will tell.

He was a soldier brave and true,
I know you will agree.
Who fought the great Rebellion
To set our country free.

He rode his snow-white charger,
As did the knights of old
With his saber by his side,
A leader brave and bold.

He led his gallant soldiers
To the beat of fife and drum,
Who with their trusty muskets,
Put the red coats on the run.

The strife was long and bitter,
And many brave men fell
To lift the yoke of bondage
From the land they loved so well.

They died to give us Liberty
From the cruel ruler's hand,
So let the bells of freedom ring
Forever in our land.

The Fishin' Hole

by Pearl Howerton

There is none so happy as a boy in June,
  When school is out and the world's in tune,
With the joys that fill a small boy's soul
  As he wanders down to the fishin' hole.

An uncrowned king, this little man
  With his fishin' worms in an old tin can,
A bent pin hook and a bamboo pole
  On his way to the fishin' hole.

No need to hurry; the fish will wait.
  He knows where there's berries by the pasture gate.
The dew is cool on his bare brown feet
  Where the berries grow so ripe and sweet.

He is a giant, ten feet tall
  Though the shadow he casts is very small;
Forgotten is school and the winter's cold
  As he wanders down to the fishin' hole.

His cheeks are brown as summer wheat;
  The world, a kingdom at his feet.
He is the heir to wealth untold
  As he dreams beside the fishin' hole.

Flour Sack Underwear

by Pearl Howerton
(January 1970)

Long ago when but a child
  There was no cash spare.
That's when my mother carefully sewed
  My flour sack underwear.

The bags that came around our flour
  Were always washed with care;
And very soon I would have
  Some brand-new underwear.

The lettering did not always fade
  But I really did not care;
It seemed to lend a bit of color
  To my flour sack underwear.

Aunt Jemima and Mother's Best
  Warmed my sturdy little chest;
Snow White provided the slip I wore
  Beneath my Sunday dress.

My nighty came down to my toes
  And wrapped around my shins.
It was very soft and snuggly
  With Robin Hood beneath my chin.

There was no lace or fancy stitches
  On my little flour sack beeches;
But Dixie Lilly, pale and neat
  Marched across my little seat.

Many years have come and gone
  Still in my dreams I see
The little flour sack underwear
  My mother made for me.

A Friend Indeed

by Pearl Howerton
dedicated to Lillian Pepmiller (February 22, 1973)

I have a friend of many years,
Who is trusted, kind, and true.
When trouble and disaster strike,
She always knows just what to do.

She does not panic or lose her head,
But promptly takes command.
And like the trooper that she is
Soon has the situation well in hand.

She is never guilty of idle gossip
But always gentle and sedate.
When the call for help arrives,
You will never find her late.

She is not frivolous nor giddy;
Like still waters, she is deep.
You may cast your troubles on her
Knowing your confidence she'll keep.

She'll do to ride the river with
And help you to keep your craft afloat.
And though the storm of life be heavy,
She will never rock the boat.

I know that God will find a place
Where the sun will always shine
In that ever-blooming garden
For this special friend of mine.

Perhaps He'll find some work for her
That would make her joy complete:
Helping some poor belated soul
Or dusting off the golden street.

The Garden

by Pearl Howerton
(March 1968)

God made Adam from a lump of clay
And rested on the seventh day;
He then took a rib from Adam's side
And created Eve, his beautiful bride.

They lived happily in the garden;
They knew no sin, nor need of pardon.
But a serpent entered the garden on day
And beguiled poor Eve, the scriptures say.

The serpent smiled and crept away;
His work was done as it is today.
Eve plucked the apple, so rosy and red,
Just above her innocent head.

They were young and the fruit was sweet;
From the Tree of Life, they both did eat.
They lived to regret it, it's sad to say;
They were driven from the garden that day.

Cast out of the garden like babes in the wood,
Without shelter and without food,
They were forced to earn their daily bread
And provide a shelter for their heads.

God did not forsake them, though they had sinned;
He gave them fields and herds to tend.
He sent the sunshine and the rain
To nourish sadly needed grain.

In the course of time, Eve bore a son;
They called him Cain, the firstborn one.
They felt that God had forgiven their sins
When He sent this precious babe to them.

Later they were given a second son
Whom they called Abel, the gentle one.
He did not care for worldly gain
As did his older brother, Cain.

He was content with his modest herd
And followed the teaching of God's Holy Word.
His herds seemed to flourish and gain each day
While Cain's seemed to sicken and dwindle away.

In a fit of anger over worldly gains
Abel by his brother was slain.
Satan had won another fight
Since the serpent entered the garden that night.

Cain was punished by the hand of God
He was banished into the Land of Nod
Where he took unto himself a wife
And lived a long and fruitful life.

The sins of the world on man has lain
Since Abel by his brother was slain,
Since our ancestor, Mother Eve
Plucked the apple from the tree.

The Ghost Tree

by Pearl Howerton

I found this tree on a windswept hill,
  Beneath the autumn sky,
Its knobby arms cast weird shadows
  On the river flowing by.

Its branches were gnarled and twisted
  By the storms of many years.
The source of its life had drained away
  Like so many bitter tears.

I felt a kindred spirit
  With this bare and dying tree.
And as I stood beside it,
  It seemed to speak to me.

I was once a mighty oak tree
  Growing strong and tall;
The monarch of the mountains
  Towering o'er one and all.

In summer I was a haven of rest
  For travelers passing by;
And the wind made golden music
  In my boughs that swept the sky.

But my limbs were withered
  By the winter's blast and chill,
Now I am a ghost tree
  On a lonely windswept hill.

Give Me a Home

by Pearl Howerton

Give me a home by the mountain stream
Where the winds blow wild and free,
Sifting the snow on the mountain tops
From time to eternity.

Give me a home by the mountain stream;
There's rest for the weary soul,
Tempest-tossed by the storm of life
While the endless ages roll.

Give me a home by the mountain stream
I would not ask for more
Than to share the beauty of the gods
Around my cabin door.

Give me a home by the mountain stream
Where the roaring eagle flies
And builds its nest on the mountain crest
Beneath the starry skies.

Give me a home by the mountain stream
Far from the haunts of men
Where the mountain peaks, their lone watch keep
Since the world began.

Let me rest beside a mountain stream
When my earthly days are o'er;
Close to God and nature
Let me sleep forever more.

God Still Lives

by Pearl Howerton
(February 1970)

Some folks say that God is dead.
How can they be so wrong?
We see Him in each blade of grass,
Hear Him in nature's song.

We see Him in each living thing
Since time was first begun—
In dewdrops on the lilies,
In gold of the morning sun.

We see Him in each lovely flower
That blooms with colors bright,
In the sun's soft warming rays,
And the pale moon's silvery light.

We see Him in the rainbow
That spans the summer sky
And in the golden hills
When autumn days are nigh.

God is here when Mother Nature
Brings forth her treasures rare
And clothes the earth with beauty
For all the world to share.

God is not dead, my doubting friends!
Just lift your eyes and see
The beauty and the wonder of the world
He made for you and me.

The Good Old Days

by Pearl Howerton

Back in the good old days
When my grandma was a girl
Their dress was very modest
And their hair was neatly curled.

Their dresses reached down to the floor
And buttoned to the chin.
Their corsets held their bosoms high
And tucked their stomachs in.

It did not matter that they couldn't breathe
Nor could they hardly feel,
Laced in this modest little jacket
Made of whale bone and of steel.

Their petticoats were many
To protect them from the breeze.
Their drawers were starched and ruffled
And reached down the knees.

When they went to church on Sunday
They looked ladylike and neat
With trailing skirts and petticoats
Wiping up the dusty street.

They knew nothing of the mini-skirt
Nor the hot pants of today.
Had they seen a lady thus attired,
They'd have fainted dead away.

Oh yes! The girls went bathing
In the good old, bygone days.
And I'm sure to them their bathing suits
Were fashion's latest craze.

Today a model would be happy
To fashion one of these
That covered up the body
And met stockings at the knees.

The good old days are gone forever.
May they never more come back
When a lady wore a king-sized bustle
Perched upon her whale-boned back.

Grandma's House

by Pearl Howerton

I like to go to Grandma's house
Because it smells so good,
Like cookies bakin' in the oven
An' the smell of burning wood.

Burnin' in the big black stove
Where she bakes her bread,
It's always better baked that way,
That's what my grandma said.

She lets me fetch the water
From the deep, cool well;
And when it's time to eat
She lets me ring the bell

To call my grandpa from the field
Where he is making hay;
It's nice to be at Grandma's house
On a sunny, summer day.

It's nice to be at Grandma's house
When the ground is white with snow;
I like the stories that she tells
Of the West so long ago.

She tells me stories of the West
When she was very young,
How her pa fought the Indians
And saw a rustler hung.

I wish I'd been a little boy
Back in my Grandma's day,
And watched her dance the minuet
When she was young and gay.

Grandmother's Wedding Wish

by Pearl Howerton
for grandson David

Young David courted the fair Eileen
And won her heart and hand
And pledged his love forever
With a golden wedding band.

With hearts aglow with love and
hope,
They stand at the crossroads of life
Starting their lifelong journey
Young David and his wife.

Listen well, my children.
This highway is wide and long.
You may gather tears and heartache
Or laughter, love, and song.

The choice is yours, my children.
Ponder it well I pray.
And gather roses instead of thorns
Along life's long highway.

Hitch your wagon to a star
And fill it with trust and love,
Faith and understanding,
And gold from the stars above.

Add some sunshine and much
laughter
And tolerance to this load.
Guard it well, my children.
And stay in the middle of the road.

Stay in the middle of life's highway
And follow where it leads.
Practice the art of give and take
With kind and loving deeds.

This road has many pitfalls—
Snares for innocent feet;
Beware of pomp and glitter
And temptations you may meet.

Grannie's Polly-Ticks

by Pearl Howerton
(September 1968)

I do declare it was a sight
What I seen on TV the other night.
Folks was fightin' like dogs and cats
At that meetin' of them Demy Crats.

It seemed they was fightin' over some planks
In some rotten old platform that some folks did say stanks.
I looked as hard as ever I could;
But I didn't see a bit of wood.

Someone hollered a big hurrah;
A man up and socked him right in the jaw.
He hit that platform with such a clank,
I'm shore he busted one of them thar planks.

Way over in the corner on a stool
A man jumped up and said,
"Now lookey here you blitherin' fool
That was my friend what you hit on the head."

Such manners they had in that there town
They wouldn't let some folks sit down.
They was all tired out, still on their feet,
Walking around tryin' to find a seat.

Such fightin' and yellin' I never seen
I thought they would bust right through that screen.
It's nice to live way out in the sticks
Away from them fightin' polly-ticks.

There wasn't many women there;
Least I couldn't see 'em anywhur.
I reckon it was no place for them,
Amongst them yellin' fightin' men.

There was woman on the stand–
Up above that roar and din.
She had come to count the votin'
For them fightin', yellin', punchin' men.

She yelled Minnesota has sixty votes;
Alabama has the same.
I think she said they've all passed out
Away up thar in Maine.

Just about then someone fell;
Above the noise I heard a man yell,
"In the name of Uncle Sam (I didn't know he was there)
Take the handcuffs off that man."

I can tell you it give me a sore,
Sittin' there in my old rockin' chair,
To see our country in such a fix
Caused by the rotten ol' polly-ticks.

In passing, I just have this to say,
"It seems we have really gone astray
From the platform our forefathers left to us
When they shed their blood to seal this trust."

The Green, Green Hills of Home

by Pearl Howerton
(August 1972)

When a youth, I often dreamed
Of lands across the sea;
I knew that fame and fortune
Were waiting there for me.

Wanderlust was in my blood
And I was bound to roam.
One sunny day, I sailed away
From the green, green hills of home.

I was young; adventure called;
Ambition was my god.
I vowed that I would carve a name
On this foreign sod.

But fortune seemed to pass me by
As o'er the world I roamed.
For my heart was left behind me
In the green, green hills of home.

In my dreams I wander back
To the hills where I was born
I see the dewdrops on the rose
And on the fields of corn.

I see the sun's bright shining face
Above the soft, green hills.
The memory of my boyhood home
Lingers with me still.

I built my castles in the air;
To me they seemed complete.
But the storms of life soon brought
them down
In ruins at my feet.

I gazed upon my shattered dreams,
My hope and courage gone;
When I heard a small voice calling
From the green, green hills of home.

I'll roam no more; I'm homeward bound
Back across the sea
Where many friends and dear ones
Are waiting there for me.

I've searched this wide world over;
O'er land and sea I've roamed.
I've found no place so fair to me
As the green, green hills of home.

The Gypsies

by Pearl Howerton
(also published under the title The Rolling Stones*)*

We Gypsies are called the rolling stones.
We gather no moss as we roll along.
The beauty we gather is wealth untold
And freedom that's dear to the gypsy's soul.

We roam the plains and desert sands;
Our campfires glow in many lands.
We are the people that God forgot.
With the rolling stones, we cast our lot.

The Gypsy's life is happy and free
Filled with laughter and song.
We know not what the morrow will bring.
But the rolling stones, roll on.

The sky is our rooftop, the ground our bed;
We barter our wares for our daily bread.
The wide road calls like a lover's song
And the Gypsies' caravan rolls along.

Do not scorn the Gypsies, my friend.
We have what you cannot buy:
The freedom of plains and rolling hills
And the blue of the summer skies.

We pitch our tents beside the road
And light our campfires bright.
And the lilting notes of the Gypsy's song
Drifts away on the silent night.

Hands

by Pearl Howerton

We write about many things
And of castles in foreign lands
But no one ever seems to write
About beautiful, helping hands:

Beautiful hands of a mother
Clasping a baby to her breast,
Soothing its childish tears away
With a gentle kind caress;

Beautiful hands that seen to whisper
Of comfort and of love,
Beautiful hands as gentle and kind
As the soft wings of a dove;

Beautiful hands that are worn and gnarled
With the work of many years,
Hands that have comforted troubled hearts
And dried a million tears;

Beautiful hands soft and white,
Beautiful hands wrinkled and old
Reaching out to help someone
Who needs a hand to hold.

Dear writers when you're writing
Of the wonders of our land
Please say a word in passing
Of these beautiful, helping hands.

Harvest Moon

by Pearl Howerton
(October 1973)

The long, hot summer is gone
And winter is drawing nigh;
The sun shines through a golden haze;
The harvest moon hangs high.

Children are starting back to school;
And the harvest is gathered in.
Golden pumpkins fill browning fields
Where the busy spider spins.

The fodder is in the shock
And the wheat is in the bin.
The squirrel is busily gathering nuts
And the cricket his chirp begins.

The apple trees in the orchard
With fruit are bending down.
Soon all the hills will blossom
With scarlet, gold, and brown.

Autumn is a sad time—
The end of a dying year.
The flowers and grasses will wither
That we have loved so dear.

But Mother Nature cares for her own;
She will fold them to her breast
And cover them with a blanket of snow
For their long winter's rest.

A Hidden Rose

by Pearl Howerton
for granddaughter Alice Duncan Fisher (January 1974)

I have a loving granddaughter
Who I often called a brat.
Now I'm ready to eat my crow
Also my proverbial hat.

She came right out of Wonderland
This little Alice of mine,
Straight from the Magic Garden
Leaving her animal friends behind.

She was a happy-go-lucky little girl.
Had this don't-care thing,
Raced through the house like a
  whirlwind,
And always let the front door bang.

She grew into a lovely maiden
Kind and good to everyone.
Leaving her don't-care world behind,
She found her place in the sun.

She is now a wife and mother
With a son and husband to adore.
When searching for the good life
Who could ask for more.

She helps her husband in his shop
Working faithfully by his side,
As fair and lovely as the day
That she became a bride.

She makes me welcome in her home
When I should chance to pass that
  way,
Treats me like an honored guest
Even tho' I'm old and gray.

Here is a word of caution
From one who really knows,
Don't judge a rosebush by its thorns
Wait till you have seen the rose.

The Hills

by Pearl Howerton

Let me live in the beautiful hills
Beside a crystal stream,
Close to God and nature
Here let me live and dream.

Dream of times in the long ago
When God in his infinite plan
Created these beautiful Ozark hills
To gladden the heart of man.

He tossed the hills and mountains
  about
And made a river or two;
He sprinkled stars like jewels bright
Up in the heavens blue.

The springtime hills are palest green
Soft as a bridal gown;
In autumn they change like magic
To yellow, red, and brown.

Pines that shade the mountain
  streams
Like gems of emerald green
Cast their shadows on the waters
Through a silvery screen.

Man has built great cities
And highways long and wide
But only God can make the trees
That grace the mountainside.

How I Would Measure A Man

by Pearl Howerton
(January 1973)

First, I would look into his heart
To find what was hidden there;
If I found love for his fellow man,
I would measure this man four
  square.

A man may measure five foot two
And the shadow he cast is small,
But measured by God's rule of life
This man may measure ten feet tall.

I would not measure a man by the
  rule
Of color nor of creed,
But by his love for his fellow man
And by his helping of those in need.

How to Get Rich Quick

by Pearl Howerton
(July 1974)

If you want to get rich quick
You must become a politician.
Money will roll in by the barrel
But it will take a lot of fixin'.

You must be a puppet on a string—
Even laugh when it ain't funny.
But remember what you want
Is to make a lot of money.

You must be a *yes* man
Who never can say *no*.
Just dance when they pull the string
And gather in lots of dough.

You will lose your self-respect
And a lot of friends it seems.
But you know what they always say,
That the end justifies the means.

When you become a politician
Trusting to your luck and fate
You will climb right up to the top
And join your friends on Watergate.

But this old gate is getting weak;
It has fought the storm so long.
So, like the others, grab a plank
And just keep holding on.

If I Could Write

by Pearl Howerton

I would write of the mighty works of God—
How He created man from a piece of sod,
And gave him freedom and power to reign
Over this beautiful, vast domain.

I would write of the great and fruitful earth
When Mother Nature has given birth
And beauty springs from her verdant breast
Over hill and plain and mountain crest.

I would write of the beauty He gave to all
Of rippling streams and waterfall
That fills the heart with melody,
Flowing serenely to the sea.

I could not write of a world at war
Nor of boys who died on a distant shore
Who valiantly fought in rain and mud
And bathed the good earth with their blood.

I could not write of battle's roar
Nor the sound of bursting shell
That turned this once-so-peaceful earth
Into a raging hell.

I could not write of a world gone mad
With lust for power and might.
It would take a mightier pen than mine
Thus I know that I cannot write.

If You Go First

by Pearl Howerton

If you go first and I go last,
Please, my dear, don't go too fast.
Don't leave me too long my way to find
For well you know that I am blind.

If you go first and I go last,
I'll dwell in the memories of the past
When we were young and life was sweet
With all our babies at our feet.

Together we've had many happy years.
We've also had our times of tears.
If you go first and I go last,
Please, my dear, don't go too fast.

And if you find you've gone too far,
Just wait for me behind a star;
When God wills, I'll come along,
Together we'll finish our journey home.

In Memory of Minnie, My Friend

by Pearl Howerton
(October 1972)

When first I knew my cousin,
She was a fair young bride
With a laughing baby boy
And a husband by her side.

She was always kind and loving—
Ruled her home with gentle grace
And always met each new-born day
With a happy, smiling face.

To know her was to love her—
My friend beyond compare,
Who had love for everyone
And always some to spare.

Many children came to her
Through those early passing years.
She has known grief and sorrow
And has had her time of tears.

When the trials of life came to her
As they do to everyone,
She just counted her many blessings
And prayed for tomorrow's sun.

Her home was always bright and cheerful;
There was no place for gloom.
And when it became too crowded
Why they just added another room.

Like ships that pass in the night,
Our families drifted apart.
But for my friend I always carried
A candle glow in my heart.

The path was rugged and rocky
On which her gentle feet had trod;
But she was ever faithful
To her family and her God.

Four score years have flown away;
My friend is here no more.
She has gone to be with loved ones
On that bright, eternal shore.

Jim and Pat

by Pearl Howerton
(September 1969)

Jim met Pat rather late in life
And knew she would make a charming wife
To grace his home and bake his bread
And soothe his ofttimes aching head.

The courtship started then and there;
Jim vowed he'd win this damsel fair.
Soon the knot was tied hard and fast;
Jim had won his lady-fair at last.

To this union Jim brought two sons;
Pat brought two sons and a lovely daughter.
The boat was heavy laden
On their matrimonial waters.

But they were brave; their hearts were true.
They knew their love would carry them through.
They set sail in the noonday sun;
Their happy voyage had just begun.

Sometimes the going was very rough
And their boat would spire about;
But Jim would steer with a steady hand
While Pat would yell and shout,

"Heave ho, my laddies, be up and about.
There's lots of work to do.
Dad is the Captain and I the mate
And you, my lads, are the crew."

These words I've heard so many times
That marriages are made in heaven.
I'm sure these words cannot apply
To a honeymoon for seven.

A Letter to Santa

by Pearl Howerton
(December 1969)

Dear Santa, I'm just a little boy
I have no money to send;
Do you have a little dog
That needs a home and a friend?

And if you do, dear Santa,
Would you bring him here to me?
And if I should be asleep
Just leave him by my tree.

He need not be a handsome dog
Nor one with a pedigree;
Just a lonely little mutt
Would do quite well for me.

A little dog with a waggly tail
And maybe a spot or two;
With shaggy hair and a loving heart,
I'm sure this kind would do.

Oh, I promise to treat him well
Keep his water bowl filled to the brim;
And sometime when he's sad,
I'll share his little house with him.

A little friend to love me
Who will never fuss nor fret,
That will let me come into his house
Even when my feet are wet.

Little Barefoot Boy

by Pearl Howerton
(January 1973)

Just to be again a barefoot boy,
A barefoot boy in spring;
To lie beneath the old apple tree
And hear the bluebirds sing.

To drive old Bossy to the meadow
Where the daisies and buttercups grow;
To hear the tinkle of her bell,
To feel the cool, soft grass between my toes.

Just to be a little barefoot boy,
Like the one I used to know,
Gay and happy the long day through
With nothing to do but grow.

Just a happy little barefoot boy
Wading in water to my knees,
Looking for crawdads in the pond,
Or watching the flight of the bumblebee.

Just to be a little barefoot boy
With a bandage on one knee,
A wisp of hair through my old straw hat,
And happy as a boy could be.

I would give the world and all its gold:
All the things that give me joy
Just to live again those carefree years
As that happy little barefoot boy.

Lonesome River

by Pearl Howerton
(August 1969)

I hear this lonesome river calling
Where are my footsteps chance to go;
I hear the music of the water
Like a drumbeat soft and low.

I hear this lonesome river calling,
"Weary pilgrim, come and rest.
Cast your burdens on the water
Of my gently flowing breast."

Drifting down this lonesome river
Leaving care and grief behind,
If I'll follow where it leads me,
Peace and comfort I shall find.

Drifting down this lonesome river
Just a weary storm-tossed soul,
Trusting that its waves will carry me
To a bright and happy goal.

Drifting down this lonesome river
When the pale moon's silver light
Lays a path across the water
In the stillness of the night.

Drifting down this lonesome river
Searching for that happy clime
I hear the rhythm of the water
Counting out the sands of time.

Drift on and on, Oh lonesome river
Carry me on your ebbing tide
Till I reach that bright forever
Far beyond the great divide.

Looking Back

by Pearl Howerton
(May 1974)

In nineteen hundred and sixteen
We entered World War One.
We thought it was the end of the world,
But our trouble had just begun.

Then came the roaring twenties,
How long ago that seems;
The twenties gave us President Hoover
And a diet of rabbit and turnip greens.

The thirties brought the Great Depression,
Unemployment for thousands of men.
The banks all closed, the money all gone,
The bottom fell out, and the roof fell in.

The thirties brought a three-years
drought,
Three years all in a row.
The vegetables withered on the vine,
Even turnip greens couldn't grow.

The thirties also gave us President Roosevelt,
Who promised a chicken in every pot,
The chicken must have flown the coop,
The pot was empty more often than not.

He gave us the C. C. Camps,
And the W. P. A.,
A man could work a few days a month,
The wage one dollar per day.

That seems so very little,
When we needed so much more,
But half a loaf is better than none,
When the wolf is at the door.

This was a sad and troubled time,
Want and depression everywhere,
But we managed to weather this storm,
Rode it out on Hope and Prayer.

Then we entered the Forties
And better times seemed in view
Then the Japs bombed Pearl Harbor,
And gave us World War Two.

Followed by Korea and Vietnam,
Warfare seemed to be our fate,
"But at last peace was declared,"
And now we have Watergate.

The famous old Watergate,
Still spinning around and around,
Its fame has spread throughout the
world,
And turned our country upside down.

It has lowered our standards in every land,
Discussed door to door,
The impact of it muddy ways,
Are felt from shore to shore.

The March Wind

by Pearl Howerton

The March wind blows and brooks overflow
Gurgling and shouting with glee,
Rolling and swelling with melting snow,
Rushing along to the sea.

The March wind blows and the mad March hare
Stays snug in his winter home,
Never wandering far afield
Till the last cold days are gone.

The March wind blows and Farmer John
Goes forth to plant his fields.
Assured by the blustery, buffeting wind
That spring is at its heels.

The March wind sighs through the slender fronds,
Of the lovely weeping willow,
Who softly slept the winter through,
A snowbank for her pillow.

The March wind lifts the dandelion
From its leafy winter bed.
With a swish and swirl its golden curls
Over the field are spread.

The March wind ruffles the mill pond
While the frog on his lily pad
Sings with the rhythm of the wind
And gaily croaks, "Not bad! Not bad!"

The March wind blows and tall trees bow
Their branches brown and bare.
Soon they'll be clothed in softest green
With robins nesting there.

The March wind blows and we know that spring
Is waiting just over the hill,
Laden with warmth and bright spring sun
To banish the winter snow's chill.

The March wind chases the fleecy clouds
Across the bright blue sky.
Gathering raindrops along the way
For April showers, by and by.

A Man of the Soil

by Pearl Howerton
for her youngest brother, Clyde Merriman (March 1970)

He was a man of the soil,
Of the good and friendly earth,
Where he spent his life, as man and boy,
From the day of his gentle birth.

He loved the hills and valleys
And the rippling waterways
Where he dreamed and roamed at will
Throughout his boyhood days.

His roots were deep and firmly planted
In the mellow sod.
He carried a dream within his heart;
And Nature was his god.

He loved the mellow earth
Where he sowed the golden grain
And watched the tender leaves unfold
In the sunshine and the rain.

He tilled the tall, green corn—
Row on never-ending row.
In the quiet of early dawn
He could almost hear it grow.

His heart was light and free
As he tilled the fertile soil.
His brow was wet with honest sweat
From days of honest toil.

He drew his substance from the earth,
His joy from all living things;
A newborn colt in the pasture,
And wild birds on the wing.

He was a man of the soil,
In tune with Nature's song.
He sleeps within the good earth now
That he had ever loved so long.

Memory Lane

by Pearl Howerton
dedicated to Hazel Pepmiller, Panama City, Florida

I often stroll down memory lane
To visit a friend I used to know
When our children played together
In the misty long ago.

It seems that only yesterday
We talked across the garden fence.
We discussed the cost of living;
A pound of coffee was fifteen cents.

I remember we voted for Herbert Hoover.
How long ago that seems.
And I am sure that never again
Will I like rabbit or turnip greens.

My little friend did not complain,
Though times were hard for everyone.
When her skies were overcast,
She always looked for tomorrow's sun.

We had many things in common
My little friend and I:
How to set the rolls to rise
Or making apple pies.

We talked of outgrown sweaters,
Of food, and balanced meals,
Of never-ending lines of socks
With runners at the heels.

Often at my kitchen door,
Her smiling face I'd see
To tell me that her dress was finished
Or to exchange a recipe.

Although we live so far apart
Oft times my thoughts take wing
And visit with my little friend
Who lives in memory lane.

The Mini Skirt

by Pearl Howerton
(1972)

We think we invented the mini skirt.
That really is not so.
This little skirt was worn by Eve
Many thousand years ago.

The beautiful Eve lived in the garden
With Adam, her loving mate.
She said, "Dear Adam, it seems to me
The spring fashions are very late!

The flowers are blooming; the birds
  are singing.
Spring is in the air.
Easter Sunday will soon be here
And I haven't a thing to wear!"

Eve found some lovely fig leaves,
So shiny, soft and green;
From these she made the mini skirt—
The first one ever seen.

She had no needles, pins, or thread,
But a great imagination!
She made and wore this little skirt
That later rocked the nation.

When Adam came home that day
He found his lovely Eve
Attired in this mini skirt
High above her knees.

He said, "My dear, it's very nice,
But grasses might be stronger;
And I think it really should
Hang down just a little longer."

Eve was lucky in a way,
Though she had no silk or linen.
For she did not have to cope
With a group of babbling women.

Eve wore this tiny, little skirt
In the misty long ago;
And if you do not believe this
Then the Bible will tell you so.

Mount Olive Church

by Pearl Howerton

Mount Olive church was built
In nineteen hundred three;
Still in my dreams I see it
As it used to be.
When a circuit rider came each month
To hold a meeting there;
People came from far and near
To this house of prayer.

This old house is silent now
Where once the community came.
I can hear the preacher say,
"Let all the people sing."
It was a happy meeting place
In the misty bygone days
Where we met each Sunday morn
To sing the hymns of praise.

The men that built Mount Olive Church
Are silent now and still.
They sleep within its shadows
On Mount Olive Hill.
The years sped by and one by one,
This lovely plot was filled
With friends and dear ones laid to rest
On Mount Olive Hill.

I often visit this silent spot
Where my friends and dear ones sleep
Safe within the friendly earth
While stars their lone watch keep.
I walk among the headstones
And read the names inscribed thereon
And vainly try to realize
The years that they've been gone.

Now around the white gravestones
The honeysuckle vines
Often drenched with teardrops
With these tears of mine.
I do not weep for those who sleep
Beneath this velvet sod
But for the sick and troubled world
That has forgotten God.

My Child

by Pearl Howerton
dedicated to Maxine Gibson for Christmas 1967

Once upon a time
A treasure came to me
A rosy laughing baby girl
As lovely as could be.

Her eyes were pools of violet;
Golden ringlets were her hair.
I think that I shall never see
A baby quite so fair.

She ruled our hearts with baby smiles
This little babe of ours—
Bound us round with bonds of love
That held like prison bars.

She grew into a happy child
That filled our home with cheer;
She seemed to grow more lovely
With each passing childhood year.

Soon school days were upon us
And my baby had to go.
The heartbreak of that first long day
I'm sure all mothers know.

Her childhood years fled quickly by
She became a maiden fair and true.
The boys came from miles around
This gentle lass to woo.

One sunny day she left our home
With the lover of her choice,
Left in our hearts a hallowed place
And the echo of her voice.

She went to grace a husband's home
Where she rules with gentle hand;
She is a queen without a crown
Who wears a wedding band.

May the gods watch over her
This precious child of mine,
And touch her very lightly
With the passing years of time.

My Dashing Grandson

by Pearl Howerton
for her grandson, Keith Rex Gibson, on his eighteenth birthday (1972)

I have a dashing grandson
Who is just eighteen years old.
The way he sweet-talks all the girls
Has never yet been told.

He has car that he calls Maude;
Why Maude I'll never know.
It seems to draw the girls about him
Wherever he may go.

There are big girls, little girls,
Girls both short and tall.
This dashing, sweet-talking grandson
Seems to charm them all.

He fills old Maude with laughing girls
And races with the wind.
And though they're shaken up a bit
They'll climb right in again.

One day he took me for a ride
In the pouring rain.
"Sightseeing," my grandson said,
But I didn't see a thing.

I was too busy holding on
To this racing, roaring Maude,
Hoping that my wig and dentures
Would not be scattered all abroad.

But he got me safely home
Back to his mother's door.
I'm sure that I will never ride
In dear old Maude anymore.

My Experience with Hoosier Nurses

by Pearl Howerton

My hospital room was a pea-soup green,
  Not a crack in the plaster to mar the scene,
But a dent in the floor, where some poor soul,
  Had cracked his skull and paid the toll,
For trusting in this haven of rest
  Which all mankind will say is the best.
Nurses in white, marching up and down,
  Looking for victims in hospital gowns,
So tie your gowns and gird them tight,
  Don't leave a speck of skin in sight,
For if you do, they're sure to spot it,
  And before you know it, Brother, you've got it.
Right in the place where it hurts the most,
  So you lie on your stomach and nibble toast,
And dream of the beautiful flowers in spring,
  Where the hop-toads wink and the birdies sing,
And the farmer sits in the shade of his barn,
  With his jug of corn liquor under his arm.
Oh, why did I leave my home in Missouri,
  And come to this land of trouble and worry
And get involved with these Hoosier nurses,
  Who carry little guns, hid in their purses,
Just awaiting a chance to blow you down,
  When you stray away from your old hometown?
They seem to have this shooting lust,
  For shoot they will; and shoot they must.
When the "Super" orders, "Fire at will,"
  One went wild and struck poor Bill,
Who meekly sat in the corner alone,
  Thinking of the comforts of home.
No time to dodge, no place to hide,
  Now he has a punctured side. "Poor soul."

Just when I thought I could take no more,
  A sweet little nurse came through the door,
With a smile on her face, like the Royal Gorge,
  And a gun in her hand like the cannon from Valley Forge.
Then stepping softly to my bed,
  "This won't hurt a bit, my dear," she said.
"Now just be calm. Oh, not so loud.
  I'll soon have you drifting on a rosy cloud."
"Drifting," she said. Boy what timing,
  I shot through the cloud with the silver lining,
Took a spin up among the stars,
  Passed by Venus, and maybe Mars,
Then fell with a thump back onto my bed,
  With a pain in my hip and a pain in my head.
Oh, woe is me, alas and alack,
  Lying prone upon my back,
Thinking of my terrible plight,
  Caused by these nurses dressed in white.
They march in pairs and in formation,
  With a smile on their faces that would conquer a nation,
With a spear in their hand and a gleam in their eye,
  Ready to smite you, hip and thigh.
When they gave me the last dose of twenty pills,
  I folded my tent and fled to the hills,
To the land of the Ozarks, and the long-eared mule,
  Where we always practice the Golden Rule.
Now you all just take it from me,
  These nurses are not all they seem to be;
Their soft, gentle hands sometimes hide thorns.
  And under their cute, little caps, I'm sure there are horns.

My Friend Johnny

by Pearl Howerton
(June 1970)

My friend Johnny is a very brave man!
Each day he meets the foe:
A sea of run-down, ailing shoes,
Row on never-ending row.

Some are run-down at the heel.
Some are slim and neat.
Some spread out like row boats
For folks with paddle feet.

He greets each patron with a smile
This patient, friendly man
And though the job looks hopeless,
He will do the best he can.

He truly keeps us on our feet
This man in our home town.
When our shoes are sad and ailing
He never lets us down.

Clickety clack the hammer goes
From the heel down to the toe.
With the skill of this ailing man
These injured shoes will walk again.

When my friend has left this world
For that home so bright and fair,
I hope that he'll find just a few
Shoes needing a bit of repair.

My Friends

by Pearl Howerton
(January 23, 1975)

I want to tell to all the world
About these friends of mine,
Without whose help and understanding
My sun would cease to shine.

For you see, I am a shut-in
And they make my life worthwhile;
Their friendship will sustain me
Till I reach that last long mile.

First there is Lillian
Whose worth cannot be told;
She is a true and trusted friend
With heart of purest gold.

Also, there is Margaret
Who is always sweet and sunny;
She sees that all my bills are paid
And tries to stretch my money.

And Dottie I must not forget
Who is very dainty and petite;
She is like a golden sunbeam
From her head down to her feet.

And Mary with her gentle smile
Is always helping those in need,
With ever-willing, serving hands,
Doing so many golden deeds.

Also I have these new friends:
Linda, Cletus, Billie, and Lou.
Who are so very special,
Although so very new.

I'm not endowed with worldly goods,
Yet I have wealth untold,
The new friends are my silver,
And the old friends are my gold.

God in his infinite mercy
Must have sent them to my door,
With friends like these around me
I could never ask for more.

Thank you, God, for all my friends
Who do so much for me.
They calm the troubled waters
On life's tempestuous sea.

My Ghost House

by Pearl Howerton
(December 1967)

This sad old house stands all alone
On a sunny grass-grown plot.
The grandeurs of its bygone years
Have long since been forgot.

Its columns once so gleaming white
Are weather-stained and brown;
Its naked windows, like unseeing
  eyes,
Gaze out upon the town.

This old house was once a home
With love and life aglow,
Where laughter rang from wall to wall
But that was long ago.

This old house is empty now,
Its life and laughter gone.
Flown away like the passing years,
Now ghosts walk there alone.

Ghosts of many happy days
Endure within this ancient home,
They once lived here long ago
Before their lives had flown.

There are ghosts of love and sorrow,
That this old house has known;
It takes all these, the poets say,
To make a house a home.

Many the brave young soldiers,
Who left this old roof tree,
To seek their fame and fortune
In lands beyond the sea.

Only the ghosts of these returned
To roam its empty halls,
To write the story of their fate
Upon its crumbling walls.

Many the great and famous men,
Who gathered behind its doors.
Only ghosts can hear the secrets now
Of those who come no more.

The ghosts that roam through this
  old house
Many a book could write
Of hopes and dreams and plans
  fulfilled
When life was young and bright.

They say that this old house must go
That progress must move along.
This relic of the past will fall,
That has graced this plot so long.

One day soon, the wreckers will
  come
To pull down columns and stone,
And close the book on this old
  house,
Where ghosts have walked so long.

My Golden Carpet

by Pearl Howerton
(September 1968)

I stand on a lovely carpet
Of falling maple leaves
That drift like golden butterflies
Upon the Autumn breeze.

My golden carpet is spread
Atop a sun-kissed hill
That in the springtime changes
To a crown of daffodils.

This wealth is all my own
To share with whom I will—
Whom I choose to visit
On my golden, sun-kissed hill.

I walk on my golden carpet
As proudly as a queen
And trade it in the springtime
For one of emerald green.

My Magic River

by Pearl Howerton

I dream of a magic river
Flowing down through the years of time.
It has no beginning or no end,
This beautiful river of mine.

It flows from the isle of nowhere
Through the land of make believe,
Where flowers bloom at midnight
And the Mockingbird sings at eve.

It flows through the land of the midnight sun,
By the land where we'll never grow old,
Where fairies dance in pale moonlight,
Waving their wands of gold.

It flows through the land of enchantment
By the castle where the princess slept,
Awaiting the prince to awake her
While her grieving parents wept.

It sings a lullaby, soft and sweet,
That lulls the soul to rest,
Rocked in the cradle of the waves,
On its gently flowing breast.

I rest beside this magic river
And weave my beautiful dreams,
Weave them of love and kindness
With threads of bright sunbeams.

I cast my dreams upon its waters,
That flow to lands unknown.
How sad I am, when I awake
To find my river is gone.

My Ozark Home

by Pearl Howerton
(in the hospital, January 1971)

I live in the beautiful Ozark hills
Where nature reigns supreme,
Close beside the rippling waters
Here let me live and dream.

How God in all His wisdom
Made the Earth, the Sea and Sky
And created these lovely Hills
For dreamers such as I.

He made the Lakes and Rivers,
The Brooklets and the Rills.
The Flowers that bloom in springtime
And the Songbirds on the hill.

On the hilltop white with hawthorn,
A castle He crafted for me,
In the springtime graced with redbud,
And the lovely dogwood tree.

I am an heir to this Kingdom.
Neither silver nor gold have I
But mine are the stars above me
And mine are the summer skies.

This wealth is mine for the taking
To share with everyone.
My diamonds are in the heavens;
And my gold in the morning sun.

The Ozark hills are my kingdom;
An uncrowned king am I.
Proudly I walk o'er my vast domain
Beneath my span of sky.

Science has put man on the moon,
And changed Niagara Falls.
But God made these lovely Ozark hills
Graced with the pine trees tall.

My Patchwork Quilt

by Pearl Howerton

My patchwork quilt that Grandma made
Has many patches of every shade;
Some are blue, and some are gold;
Some have roses, gay and bold.

Some are like the sky at morn;
Some the color of soft green corn;
All sewn together in a lovely lilt
Marching across my patchwork quilt.

Each patch tells a story of someone's life;
Some of joy, and some of strife;
Where love and sorrow go hand in hand,
Sewn in each patch of this patchwork land.

This silvery grey was Cousin Ann's,
Who sailed away to distant lands;
To teach the heathen how to pray
And worship God, as we do today.

The blue was Mother's, for her very first date
That she wore to a party and stayed out late.
It seemed that way to my Grandma then;
Though Mother said, "It was only ten."

It seems I can see my Grandma now;
With trembly hand and furrowed brow;
Patiently plying her needle and thread;
Sewing this coverlet for my bed.

When the nights are dark and winds blow cold;
I snuggle down beneath its folds;
Safe from darkness and childish fear,
It seems to bring my grandma near.

My Pot of Gold

by Pearl Howerton
(June 9, 1971)

When a child, I was often told
At the rainbow's end was a pot of gold;
And if I watched and searched with care
I might someday find it there.

This dream I carried through the years—
It gave me hope and calmed my fears,
It warmed me when the nights were cold—
Just dreaming of my pot of gold.

I left my home and loved ones there;
I promised them my gold to share.
And when I found the rainbow's end,
I'd come back home to them again.

I chased the rainbow through the sky
While life and youth were passing by.
I had no time for love or friends
Searching for the rainbow's end.

I searched the mountains, deserts, plains;
I crossed the ocean and back again,
Through burning heat and winter's cold—
Searching for my pot of gold.

I'm growing old; my steps are slow.
I know I have not long to go.
And now when life is almost done,
I've found my Gold in the evening sun.

My Prayer

by Pearl Howerton

Lord, give me courage to bear this blight,
Slowly blotting out the light.
When I must walk in darkness alone,
Please, dear Lord, don't let it be long.

Don't let it be long, dear Lord, I pray
When I cannot see the light of day.
And hold my hand, lest un aware,
I sink in quicksand and despair.

Let me hold in my heart the beauties I've seen,
Of soft spring days, and meadows green.
Sprinkled with dewdrops and fairy's lace,
And the smiles and tears on a baby's face.

The beauty of rainbows, after the rain,
And ripening fields of golden grain,
These I would cherish when sight is gone.
But please, dear Lord, don't let it be long.

You who are strong and full of grace,
Please help me keep a smiling face.
And in my heart, help me keep a song,
When the days grow dark and long.

My Prison

by Pearl Howerton
(July 1968)

I live in a darkened prison
And count the endless hours
That pass so slowly before me
As myriad as the stars.

This prison in which I live
Has neither bars nor walls.
Yet I cannot welcome the sunrise
Nor see the twilight fall.

In my dreams I wander back
To the time when life was sweet,
With Nature's beauties all about me
Like trophies at my feet.

I see the snow-capped mountains,
The white clouds drifting by,
Lambs in the greening meadows,
And the blue of summer skies.

I see the shimmering rainbow
Just after a summer rain,
The Ozark hills and forests,
And fields of golden grain.

I have music in my prison
Composed by my feathered friends;
The cheerful song of the mockingbird
And the gentle peep of the wrens.

The coo of a dove at early morn,
The whippoorwill's lonely call,
The merry whistle of the bobwhite quail,
Down by the garden wall.

These treasures I've stored within my heart
And cherish them one by one.
They are my light, my guiding star,
My rainbow and my sun.

I live in a darkened prison;
God's beauties no longer I see.
Someday the gate will be opened
And I shall then be free.

God holds the key to my prison;
One day he will open the door,
And call me from this world of darkness
To that bright eternal shore.

My Rock 'N Roll Queen

by Pearl Howerton

My gal Sal is a rock 'n roll queen.
The things she can't do are yet to be seen.
She wears her little mini skirt well above her knees
When she shakes that wicked shimmy in the evening breeze.

Sal in long and skinny and her knees they sort 'o knock;
But let me tell you brother, she can really roll 'n rock.
She can do the little doggie, the swim and the crawl.
But the way she shakes that shimmy really beats them all.

She can do the boogie woogie and the jitter bug;
When Sal goes into action she can really cut the rug.
She rocks and she rolls from her head to her knees;
When she shakes that wicked shimmy in the evening breeze.

My Street

by Pearl Howerton
(January 1969)

I have a favorite street
Where I walk 'most every day
And try to read the faces
I meet along the way.

Some are young and some are old;
Some are bright and gay,
All rushing onward into life
Along this broad highway.

There are many kinds of houses
Along this busy, bustling street.
Some are old and some are new
And some are incomplete.

The little one is a friendly house.
It seems to wear a smile
Inviting the weary stranger,
"Come in, and rest a while."

Its walls are bright and shining;
Its windows wear a glow,
In the happy bloom of springtime
Or in the winter's snow.

And then, there is the big house
Upon the highest hill.
When I pass its shuttered face,
I feel an inward chill.

It has a proud and haughty look,
A look of wealth and fame.
Where the milk of human kindness
And love are but a name.

And then, there is the cottage
Set on its velvet lawn
Just bursting out with gladness
To greet each early dawn.

I see a smiling, happy mother
Busily laying the evening meal
And rosy-cheeked, laughing children
With puppies at their heels.

And so the homes along my street
Many a story tell
Of love and life and mirth and woe
That behind their portals dwell.

My Valley

by Pearl Howerton

I dream of a beautiful valley,
Hid away in the soft green hills,
Where the magic beauty of sight and
 sound,
My heart with rapture fills.

Let he who will, seek the cities
Paved streets and buildings high;
But give me this beautiful valley
With hills that reach the sky.

Hills that in autumn are painted
With colors of every hue,
And leaves that are tipped with diamonds,
Kissed by morning dew.

When the sun comes over the hilltop,
And the stars roll back in the night,
This beautiful valley is flooded
With showers of golden light;

Falling on glade and meadow
That sway in the morning breeze,
Touched by the gentle south wind,
As it whispers among the trees.

Trees that crown the hilltop,
Where the mocking bird builds her
 nest,
Are casting their purple shadows,
Inviting the traveler to rest.

A haven of rest for the traveler,
Upon the highway of life,
In search of a bright tomorrow,
Where cometh no troubles and strife.

Let me rest a while in this valley,
Ere my days on earth are done,
And I start my last, long journey,
To the land of the setting sun.

When twilight dims the hilltop,
And the evening shadows fall,
This valley is wrapped in slumber,
And God watches over all.

My Wildwood Rose

by Pearl Howerton

I found my love in the mountains
With sun on her golden hair.
I knew that only the hand of God
Could make a flower as fair.

I called her my wildwood rose
And won her for my own.
In the beauty of the Ozark hills
We made our little home.

Our life was full and happy
And our love was pure and sweet.
She was lovely as the flowers
That blossomed at her feet.

But like the flowers she faded
And the angels came one day.
Now my love is sleeping
Beneath a mound of clay.

My mountain home is empty
Sad and lonely are my days,
Since my wildwood flower sleeps
Beneath a mound of clay.

My Woodland Nymph

by Pearl Howerton
for granddaughter Bonnie Lou Gibson Risby in 1954

For Bonnie, My Sunny-faced Lover
Smiling through life she goes,
Filled with laughter and sunshine,
From her head right down to her toes.

She's like an elf in the woodland,
Who has the ear of a fawn,
That will bring her joy and gladness,
As the years go rolling on.

Her eyes are blue as the Heavens,
Her hair is the softest brown,
Her face is like a sun-kissed pool,
That never wore a frown.

She is never cross or frowning,
As she meets each newborn day,
But scatters joy and sunshine,
Although the skies are gray.

This little Maid was Heaven-sent,
To bring joy to her home,
And all the friends who know her
Wherever they may roam.

This is a wish from her Grandma,
Who's writing this little rhyme,
May she dance on a golden rainbow,
Right down to the end of time.

Nancy

by Pearl Howerton
for granddaughter Nancy Duncan Brock

This is my lovely grandchild
Of whom I'm very proud;
The thoughts she puts into my head
I dare not speak aloud.

Her eyes are bright as morning sun
Her hair like the raven's wing,
And all the lads for miles around
Are shackled with her chain.

She's like a sly, sleek pussy cat,
Though I can see no flaws.
But don't forget there's needle points
Hidden in her velvet paws.

Her face is like a lovely dream
Her head is like a rock,
But when the laddies gaze at her
Their knees begin to knock.

They come to worship at her shrine
These poor deluded swain;
And though she frowns upon them
They venture back again.

I'm just her doting grandma
And perhaps a silly fool;
But I'd like to bend her o'er my knee
And apply the golden rule–er.

New Friends

by Pearl Howerton
an unfinished poem for Don Schmidt of La Crosse, Wisconsin (1969)

One day while walking down the street
I passed *Don's Seldom Inn.*
Says I, "I'll stop and sit a while
And have a glass of gin."

There I found two fair young maids
Who were really getting tight.
Ruby was crying in her beer
And singing "Good Night, Irene Good Night."

Irene says, "Now listen here
Who want to go to bed?
Let's have another glass of beer
And paint this old town red.

We'll let the party start right here
And dance around the clock.
Let these fogies talk all night.
Who are they to mock.

The New Moon

by Pearl Howerton

The lovely, untouched moon
Hung a million years in space,
Till man in all his wisdom
Put footprints on its face.

The moon that was a lover's dream
Will never be the same,
To those who walk in tender light
Down there on lover's lane.

The romance and the mystery
From our lovely moon is gone,
We find it's made of sand and ash
And rather plain volcanic stone.

Gone also is the man in the moon,
Along with his moldy cheese,
We have instead our nation's flag
Showing what science can achieve.

Astronauts plant the Stars and Stripes
Upon the moon's rugged face,
May its colors endure forever
On lunar soil and outer space.

They say we'll visit on the moon
In a dozen years or so,
Just let me linger here on earth
Basking in its mellow glow.

The New Year

by Pearl Howerton
(January 1, 1973)

Old Father Time has given us
Another bright new year.
Will it bring us peace on earth?
Or bring more grief and fear?

As did the many years gone by
Filled with pain and woe
When our sons were called to war
And we had to see them go.

They were called to fight in foreign lands
A war they could not win.
Now they are only shadowy ghosts
In a world that might have been.

Before this new year passes by
Many more will die in vain
That men may fill their greedy tills
With their ill-gotten gain.

Do the blood-stained dollars in your till
Ever haunt you in your sleep;
While the ghosts of dying soldier boys
Beg for mercy at your feet?

Please tell me, Mister Warlord,
Safely hidden in your lair
How much blood does it really take
To make a millionaire?

How much blood does it really take
To make a millionaire?

October

by Pearl Howerton

October days are here again;
Fodder's in the shock, wheat's in the bin.

The apples are gathered and stored with care,
Along with hickory nuts for all to share.

Golden pumpkins in the corn fields lay,
That will be Jack-o-lanterns on Halloween day.

Funny faces and coal-black cats,
Little green men with pointed hats,

Ghosts and ghouls that roam at night,
Dragging their chains in the pale moonlight.

There are goblins, elves and witches too,
Cooking up their powerful brew.

Ere she sails away on her famous broom,
To sweep the cobwebs off the moon.

Said the wise old witch, I do believe,
This moon is made of cheddar cheese;

I think I'll stop and take a bite,
Before I fly back to earth tonight.

The Old Courthouse

by Pearl Howerton

They say the council met last night
To determine the fate of a very old
friend
That stands so old and helpless
Before this circle of powerful men.

This old house has been condemned;
Its useful days are gone.
It must give way to modern times;
Progress must move on.

This old structure has housed the Courts
For four score years and ten
Where Judge and Jury meted out
Justice to all men.

Its pillars once so gleaming white
Are weathered now and brown,
Its windows like all-seeing eyes
Gaze out upon our town.

This old house so scarred and worn,
They say it must come down.
But in that misty long ago
'Twas the showplace of our town.

The men who built this old
courthouse
Have long since passed away;
But there are some who still
remember it
In its nobler, grander days.

The lofty maples spread cooling shade
Over yard and old stone wall
Where oldsters meet to chat awhile
While the evening shadows fall.

This old relic of the county
Folks say that it now must go.
Its memory will live in many hearts
When man's progress lays it low.

One day soon, a crew will come
To pull down stones and bricks of
brown.
And we'll bid, "Adieu Old Courthouse,
You have loyally served our town."

The Old Log House

by Pearl Howerton

The old log house is where I was born
And spent my boyhood years,
Sheltered from the storms of life,
From childish griefs and fears.

Where we gathered 'round the open fire
On stormy winter nights,
Safe within its sturdy walls
When the ground with snow was white.

My mother, then so young and fair
Was often seated at her loom.
The shuttle in her nimble hand
Seemed to hum a tune.

Over and under, over and back
Each carrying a tiny thread
That soon might be a tablecloth
Or a coverlet for my bed.

I watched her spin the golden flax
On her little spinning wheel.
Fine linen thread to warp the loom,
With cashmere wool to fill.

Linsey-Woolsey for her dress
Which she wore with greatest pride
To the village church on Sunday
With Father by her side.

Years have come and years have gone.
My parents are here no more.
But the flowers my mother planted
Still bloom around the door.

I'm growing old and feeble now,
Past three score years and ten
Spent ever near that old log house
Wherein my life began.

The Old Missouri Hills

by Pearl Howerton

I want to wander back to the old Missouri hills.
The old familiar places linger with me still.
Just to hear my mother's voice would give my heart a thrill
And to hear the mocking birds on the old Missouri hills.

I want to wander back to the old Missouri hills,
Hear the rippling waters fall and the music of the rills.
Just to see the snowy hawthorn and hear the whippoorwills
When the evening shadows fall on the old Missouri hills.

I want to wander back to the old Missouri hills,
To walk along the stream beside the old water mill.
Just to see the miller pouring golden grain into the till
And to see the dogwoods bloom on the old Missouri hills.

I want to wander back to the old Missouri hills.
In the haunts of childhood, I want to linger still.
Just to see again the schoolyard where I played with Tom and Bill.
Where the old schoolmaster sleeps in the shadow of the hills.

Our Handy Andy Gal

by Pearl Howerton
(August 1970 – Lillian Pepmiller)

There is a gal in our town
Who is busy as can be.
She lends a hand to everyone
Even to a bum like me.

She gets up early in the morning
And works from sun to sun.
She holds on like a bulldog
Until the job is done.

She is full of vim and vigor.
Her steps are never slow.
When her helpers lag behind,
She yells, "Get up and go."

Armed with her little hatchet,
Destruction is her aim.
The work she turns out everyday
Would put a man to shame.

If you have some brush to cut
And your Bush Hog isn't handy,
Just call this spunky little gal
With her Handy Andy

No, I will not tell her name;
But I'll give you a little clue:
She works at the PN office.**
The guess is up to you.

**PN office, the *Prospect News* office

Over the Tide

by Pearl Howerton

Sing of the beautiful home on high
Far across the great divide.
My savior awaits to pilot me home
Across the raging tide.

Chorus
Carry me over the raging tide,
Carry me over the tide.
Jesus, reach down your hand to me
And carry me over the tide.

Sing of the beautiful home on high
Where the streets are paved with gold,
Where we'll live with Christ forever
In the Land where we'll never grow old.

Chorus
Carry me over the raging tide,
Carry me over the tide.
Jesus, reach down your hand to me
And carry me over the tide.

Sing of the beautiful home above
Where God on his snow-white throne,
Patiently waits with arms of Love
To gather his children home.

Chorus
Carry me over the raging tide,
Carry me over the tide.
Jesus, reach down your hand to me
And carry me over the tide.

The Ozark Plane and I

by Pearl Howerton
(July 1972)

I always said I never would ride
On one of them there Airo-planes.
I thought if God meant us to fly
He would have given us some wings.

When I had to make a trip
Either by bus or train,
My children always said to me,
"Ma, why not take an Ozark Plane?"

So they took me to the airport.
To see I was scared, was plain.
There it was on the runway—
That shiny Ozark Plane.

It took a heap of courage
To climb them little stairs.
My knees were awful shaky.
So I said a little prayer.

The folks already on the plane
Was calm as they could be.
No one seemed scared a bit—
That is no one but me.

I sat there holdin' to my chair
As scared as scared could be.
I said, "O Lord, I know I'm a fool
But please watch over me."

Soon a voice from somewhere said,
"We are now up in the air."
Right then I wished that I was home
In my faithful rockin' chair.

There I was flying through the air
Just like a bird on the wing.
I know that I will never forget
My first ride on an Ozark Plane.

The Ozarks

by Pearl Howerton

When nature went looking for a garden spot,
She stopped in the Ozark Hills.
And spread her beauty with a lavish hand,
Over forest, lakes, and rills.

She clothed the hills with emerald green,
Mountains, she crowned with snow.
And set to music, the mountain streams,
Where the rippling waters flow.

She waved her wand over hill and plain,
That bloom with beauty bright,
Put a song in the throat of the mocking bird,
That sings in the morning light.

She touched the rivers with magic,
That mirror the mountain crest.
And waterfalls like a bridal gown,
Tossed on her flowing breast.

She called it the garden of the gods,
Where she still reigns supreme,
And ruffles the waters of the lakes
With her silvery screen.

This legend has been handed down,
A thousand years or more,
And the beauties of the Ozarks,
Have been sung from shore to shore.

Ozarks Calling

by Pearl Howerton
(March 1968)

Don't you hear the Ozarks calling,
"Weary pilgrim, come and rest;
Rest beside my rippling waters,
With nature at its best."

Don't you hear the Ozarks calling,
Where the wind blows wild and free,
And the voice of Nature's singing,
Through every bush and tree?

Don't you hear the Ozarks calling,
From the garden of the gods
From the hills and lofty mountains,
Where no man's feet have trod?

Don't you hear the Ozarks calling,
When the hills with snow are white,
And the pine trees softly whisper,
In the stillness of the night?

Don't you hear the Ozarks calling,
"I have treasures enough to spare;
Drink freely of my healing waters,
Breathe my unpolluted air."

Don't you hear the Ozarks calling,
In the gentle voice of spring,
When songbirds sing in chorus,
That makes the welkin ring.

Don't you hear the Ozarks calling,
When the summer moon is white,
When the voice of Nature whispers
In the silence of the night?

Don't you hear the Ozarks calling,
When the hills are red and gold
Offered by the Master Painter
When His canvas He unfolds:

Don't you hear the Ozarks calling,
With a clear and gentle voice,
"All my beauties are God-given;
Of His treasures, take your choice."

Pearl's Last Poem

by Pearl Howerton

Following is the last poem Grandma Pearl Howerton wrote.
It was published in the *Prospect News* along with her obituary.
She asked Dottie Hunsaker to see that it was published at her death.

Don't let it be long, dear Lord, I pray
For when no longer I see the light of day.

And hold my hand lest unaware
I sink in quicksand and despair.

Let me hold in my heart the beauties I've seen
Of rolling hills and meadows green,

Sprinkled with dewdrops and fairies' lace
Like smiles and tears on a baby's face.

In my heart let me keep a song
When my last days grow dark and long.

The Piney Wood Hills

by Pearl Howerton

One summer day I lost my way
While searching for a still.
Instead I found a lovely maid
There in the piney wood hills.

She was standing beside the river
With a shotgun in her hands.
She said, "What are you doing
Here on my father's land?

If you are a Revenuer,
Mister, you'd better run.
Some things I don't know about;
But I know how to use this gun."

"Miss, I'll try to tell you
If you'll put that big gun down.
I could not run if I wanted to;
My feet are frozen to the ground."

With that gun pointed straight at me,
She looked so small and sweet,
My heart just took a tumble
And fell right at her feet.

"If you will only listen,
I will explain to you,
I'm a stranger in these hills;
And I am only passing through."

Lowering her big gun to the ground
And offered me her hand.
"If you are not a Revenuer,
You are welcome on our land."

She said, "I'm sorry I was rude.
And my name is Jill.
I live beside the river
In these piney wood hills."

I was no longer a Revenuer.
And forgotten was the still.
I lost my heart beside the river
To a little girl named Jill.

We wandered through the piney wood hills,
Fished in the rippling streams,
Among her native wildflowers,
We built our hopes and dreams.

Along the creeks and through the hills,
We wandered side by side.
In the shadow of the pines,
She promised to be my bride.

We were married in the autumn
When the harvest moon was mellow gold.
This wildwood flower now is mine
Forever to have and to hold.

I bless the day I lost my way
While searching for a still,
And found this lovely wildwood flower
Down in thc piney wood hills.

The Question Box

by Pearl Howerton
for her great grandson, Robert Breidecker

I know a curious little boy
Who is always asking "Why?"
Why flowers bloom in the summer time,
And in the winter die?

He wants to know who made the trees,
And why the earth is round,
Why do the birds fly in the air
And snakes crawl on the ground?

He wants to know why birds have feathers
And why the cat has hair;
Why Grandma always falls asleep
In her old Rocking Chair?

He wants to know who made the sun
And where is goes at night;
Why does water run downhill;
And why the snow is white?

He wants to know why skies are blue
And what holds up the stars;
How do the little fireflies know
When to light their fires?

He wants to know why milk is white
When the cow is red?
Why the doctor brings the baby
When Mama's sick in bed?

He wants to know why he gets punished
When sister has been bad
And why it is that Santa Claus
Looks so much like Dad?

I tell you what, this question box
Has me in a spin.
When I think he's all run down
He starts right up again.

The Raggedy Man

by Pearl Howerton
also titled A Boy's Dream (1966)

When I grow up I'm gonna be
The nicest old Raggedy Man you ever did see.
I'll sit in the sun wherever I choose
And wiggle my toes in my raggedy shoes.
I won't have to wash my hands or clean my feet
Every time I go in to eat.

When I get to be a Raggedy Man
I won't have to run errands for my sister Ann
Or hear Ma holler, "Johnny, come here.
Brush you teeth and comb you hair.
Mind your manners and be polite,
We're having guests for dinner tonight."

"Sit up straight; don't slump in your chair;
And please don't pull Samantha's hair.
Say yes ma'am, no ma'am, Thank you ma'am, please.
And cover your mouth when you have to sneeze."

When I get to be a Raggedy Man
I'll eat my meals from an old tin pan.
Won't have to sit up straight or wear fine clothes,
Or squeaky new shoes that hurt my toes.

When I'm a Raggedy Man, I'll do as I please.
I'll wade in the water right up to my knees.
I'll whistle and sing as I walk down the street
And ask in to dinner all the kids that I meet.
I'll tell them stories of Goblins and Elves
And wiggle-cum-squiggles that swallow themselves.

Of old John Silver with his wooden leg,
And Spanish Gold hid in a keg,
Of the mean old dragon with his flaming tongue,
And Captain Bligh who the pirates hung,
I'll tell of the treasure that's said to be,
In Davey Jones' locker under the sea.

Then I'll tell them the story I like best
Of fifteen men on a dead man's chest
Singing, "yo ho ho and a bottle of rum,"
While the Devil ran away with rest.
Oh I'll make kids happy as ever I can
When I get to be a Raggedly Man—
Just a nice old Raggedy, Raggedy Man.

The Rain

by Pearl Howerton

When the skies are dark and gray
And rain is falling by the hour,
I just close my eyes and see
Greening fields and blooming flowers.

I see the mighty oak tree
Put on her new spring dress
And make a shelter in her boughs
For singing birds to nest.

When the rain is gently falling
On the brown and fertile earth,
It is preparing Mother Nature
To give her yearly, fruitful birth.

If we did not have the rain,
All things would cease to grow.
The mighty forests would vanish
And the rivers cease to flow.

We need the sunshine and the rain.
We can't have one and not the other.
It is against God's all-wise plan
For He is nature's greatest lover.

God in His infinite wisdom
Portions out the sunshine and the rain,
That each might fall when needed
If we are to harvest golden grain.

Raindrops

by Pearl Howerton
(June 9, 1971)

I hear the raindrops gently falling
  On my window pane;
In the stillness of the night,
  They sing a sweet refrain.

When all the world is sleeping
  They sing a lullaby—
Soft as the tears of angels
  Falling from the sky.

Some say they do not like the rain;
  For them it spoils the day.
I see promises of springtime beauty
  When the skies are gray.

I see the purple violets rise
  From their wintery bed,
Daffodils and dandelions
  Raise their golden heads.

I see the meadow grasses
  Putting on cloaks of green,
Buttercups and daisies
  By the rippling stream.

When I hear the raindrops falling
  On my window sill,
It's not raining rain to me—
  It's raining daffodils.

Let the raindrops gently fall
  On my window pane tonight
Wrapping me in peaceful slumber
  Until the morning light.

The Rainy Day

by Pearl Howerton
(June 1968)

On a rainy day I like to walk
And hear the raindrops softly talk
To the flowers and grasses at my feet
And march like soldiers down the
street.

They dance before me on the walk
And on the garden wall;
The raindrops play a lovely tune
Upon my parasol.

I like the feel of a rainy day
When the air is pure and sweet;
To see the thirsty flowers drink
Makes my day complete.

On a rainy day, I like to think
On God's more wondrous plan—
How He portioned the sunshine and
the rain
To gladden the heart of man.

I like to walk on a rainy day
And breathe the pure, clean air
And see the flowers lift their heads
With freshness everywhere.

The raindrops are my special friends;
We take many walks together.
We wander o'er the meadows green
And through the fields of heather.

The skies are never gray to me;
I see roses blooming there,
The colors of the rainbow,
And blossoms sweet and fair.

I seem to hear the raindrops talking
To the seedlings at my feet,
That have slept throughout the winter
Beneath their snow-white sheet.

I wander home refreshed and calm
At the close of a rainy day,
Fold my walls about me
And shut my cares away.

My friendly walls enfold me
In a gentle warm embrace
And tell me that tomorrow
The sun will show its face.

Red Roses

by Pearl Howerton

My love gave me red roses
Fresh as the morning dew;
He promised that his love for me
Would be forever true.

They sparkled with the dew drops
And he placed them in my hand.
And our lives we bound together
With a golden wedding band.

We made a home together
Close by the rippling stream.
There in our little cottage
We built our hopes and dreams.

He vowed his love for me was true—
True as the stars above
And we'd keep the roses blooming
On the altar of our love.

But a shadow came between us;
I felt his love grow cold.
Now I live alone in sorrow;
Our love, I could not hold.

He left me for another;
I knew my life was o'er.
Now the roses bloom no longer
Around the cottage door.

I saw my roses fading
In the noonday sun.
And I watched the petals falling—
Falling one by one.

My life is ever lonely.
My days are dark and long.
Now I walk alone in darkness
Since my love is gone.

In my heart I hold a memory
Of a love I thought was true.
In my hand the thorny branches
On which the roses grew.

The Ridge Road

by Pearl Howerton
(October 1968)

This road is but a winding trail,
Around the river's bend;
To some it's just a lovely road,
But to me it is a friend.

A friend that greets me twice a year,
In the fall and in the spring;
When colors dot the roadside,
Like beads upon a string.

In the spring this road is edged
With fronds of softest green,
Where clouds of snowy hawthorn
And dogwood may be seen.

I pass this way in autumn,
When the leaves are tinged with red;
Where the winds ring bells of music,
In the boughs above my head.

I stand upon the highest peak,
Where the winds blow wild and free
High above the rolling river,
Rushing onward to the sea.

From this lofty vantage point,
I view the works of men;
But the beauty of the ridge road,
Was made by an unseen Hand.

The Hand of a Master Painter,
That wields a magic brush;
Leaving gems of beauty,
With every gentle touch.

When it's autumn in the country
With nature at its best,
The ridge road flames with color
Up to the topmost crest.

The beauty of the ridge road,
Is in my heart to stay;
I may not pass this way again,
Till spring is on its way.

The Rosebud

by Pearl Howerton
to Jim and Pat (June 1970)

A symbol of eternal love—
The flower of lovely grace—
Keep on the altar of your love
A rosebud in the vase.

Life's not a bed of roses;
We would not have it so.
But roses given by loving hands
Will keep the heart aglow.

When skies are dark and overcast,
You feel you've lost the race;
Just count your blessings one by one
And put a rosebud in the vase.

When you are feeling sad and blue
And life's not worth the while,
Just think of roses in your vase
And give the world a smile.

Just keep a rose forever blooming
Upon the alar of your heart.
And when the storms of life assail you,
Your love will ne'er depart.

The Rover

by Pearl Howerton
(August 1970)

My lover was a rover.
The highway was his home.
He said if I would wed him,
He would cease to roam.
He vowed to always love me
And leave me never more.
He would plant some roses
Round the cottage door.

We settled down in Texas
Close by the long highway;
Our life was gay and happy
For many sunny days.
But his gypsy blood kept calling.
I knew he had to roam.
For the rolling highway
Was his home, sweet home.

One summer day he left me
Beside our cottage door.
I knew our life was over;
I'd see him nevermore.
For the highway was his mistress;
They travel hand in hand.
They'll roam the world together—
The highway and my man.

Santa

by Pearl Howerton

Christmas Eve is coming soon
And snow is in the air;
Soon Santa will be bringing gifts
To children everywhere.

He called out to his helpers,
"Go fetch my reindeer eight.
Make haste and fill my sleigh tonight
For Santa must not be late."

The sleigh was filled to overflowing
With airplanes, trucks, and sleds,
Dolls, picture books, and games,
Candy, nuts, and apples red.

The reindeer led by Rudolph
Seemed to know just where to go;
They never missed a single child
While speeding through the snow.

He visits the mansion on the hill,
The humble cottage small;
Santa knows no creed nor color
He is a friend to all.

Bright-eyed children watch and listen
Their stockings hang in a row,
For the sound of Santa's sleigh bells
Through the drifting snow.

On Christmas Day the bells will ring
With glad tidings and good cheer
Peace on earth, good will to men
Throughout the coming year.

The Sea of Life

by Pearl Howerton

As babes, we are cast on the sea of life
To weather its troublesome waves;
We struggle to keep our craft afloat
From the cradle to the grave.

The strong will conquer the storms of life;
The weak will fall by the way,
Strewn like driftwood along the shore
Washed by the ocean's spray.

Life is what we make it
I've heard the wise men say,
But the hand of destiny charters the course
We sail from day to day.

The sea of life is wide and long
We ride its crest with a smile,
Till destiny turns our craft about
And life is not worthwhile.

We are but pawns in the game of life
Played by the hand of fate.
Sometimes we make the move that's right
Sometimes we move too late.

Fate points our sails to the westward sun
When the pawn grow weak and old;
We are not the masters of our fate
Nor the captains of our soul.

The Silent Friend

by Pearl Howerton
(January 1969)

He who has a book
Will always have a friend.
Just open the pages and you'll find
Companionship within.

When all your dreams are shattered
And your world seems all askew,
Just turn the pages of a book
And see the light come through.

This friend is always willing
To travel at your side.
It will take you to the mountaintop
Or on the ocean wide.

You may follow the gypsies' caravans
Through the desert's burning sand,
Build a castle in the air
In some far and distant land.

And if you like adventure,
You may sail the bounding main,
Walk through crumbling castles,
Or fight a bull in Spain.

This friend will take you into orbit
Around Venus, the moon, or Mars.
You may walk along the Milky Way
And count ten million stars.

With this friend beside you
To open all the doors,
You may search for hidden treasures
On the ocean's coral floors.

When your troubles have you down,
Sunk up to your chin,
Just open the pages of a book
And let the sunshine in.

It will lift the darkest cloud.
So why sit sadly pining?
Just open up your favorite book
And find the silver lining.

He who has a book
Is never quite alone.
Friends found within its pages stay
When human friends are gone.

The South Wind

by Pearl Howerton

I love the balmy south wind;
It softly speaks to me
Of lovely scenes and places
Far across the sea.

When I am tired and weary,
It lulls my soul to rest
Flowing gently o'er my cheek
Like a fond caress.

It sways the weeping willow
Like dancers on the floor;
Then very quietly steals away
Softly tapping on each door.

It soothes the weary traveler
With sweat upon his brow,
Makes golden music in the trees
Up to the topmost bough.

It sails the white and fleecy clouds
Across the summer sky.
When the leaves are dancing,
South Wind is passing by.

Oh take me with you, South Wind,
Across the ocean wide,
O'er lofty hills and mountains,
And o'er the Great Divide.

Where flowers bloom forever
And stars their lone watch keep
Then gently fold me in your arms
And lay me down to sleep.

Spring

by Pearl Howerton

Spring brings warming sun and rain
Clothing in beauty hill and plain,
Spreading a carpet of softest green
Where daisies and buttercups may be seen.

Daffodil and crocus just peeping through,
And violets drenched in morning dew,
The pussy willow with her kittens small,
And roses blooming by the wall.

Hear the soft wind murmur through bush and tree,
And the drowsy hum of the honey bee,
As it busily flits from flower to flower
Gathering nectars each garden hour.

The bobwhite calls to his little mate,
Safe on her nest by the garden gate.
Lambs in the meadow and birds on the wing—
Everything seems to shout, "Now it's SPRING!"

Boys in the meadow flying kites so high
Chasing the white clouds out of the sky.
Tie your worries to the tail of a kite
And watch them soar right out of sight.

No time for worry, doubt, or fear;
It's time to be happy. Spring is here.
"Come on out and race with me,"
Says the laughing brook on its way to the sea.

Spring Is Here

by Pearl Howerton
(February 1968)

Spring is here! The beautiful spring!
Awake and let the joy-bells ring!
Give thanks to the maker of all living things,
Who gives to us this glorious spring!

Spring is here! And sap runs high,
In branch and bough that reach for the sky,
Leaves unfold. And palest green
Carpets the meadow by the freshening stream.

Spring is here! No longer doubt it.
All growing things seem to shout it.
Lambs in the meadow and birds on the wing
Heralding in the beautiful spring.

Mother Nature, so old and wise,
Cast off her blanket of snow.
And bids her sleeping children, "Arise!
Awake, it is time to grow."

Then she steps forth, with magic wand,
To direct the chorus down in the pond,
Where each croaking frog, in his spotted vest
Valiantly tries to out-croak the rest.

Spring is here! And the whippoorwill
Sends his mournful cry from over the hill.
The turtle dove in her cloak of gray,
Coos to her lover over the way.

Spring is here! And the babbling brook
That carries away the snow,
Seems to catch the spirit of spring
In her rushing, rippling flow.

Spring is here! And the dandelions
Lift golden sleepy heads,
Drowsy from cold winter's sleep,
Snuggled down in leafy beds.

The warm sun shines through a golden screen,
Falling on daisy and rose,
Warming the bed where violets sleep,
Down to their purple toes.

Spring is here! With beauty sublime
Beauty not made by man,
But wrought by the touch of a magic brush
In the master painter's hand.

Spring is here! The beautiful spring!
Let all the world awake and sing!
Pick up the melody of nature's song,
And make the welkin ring!

Spring is here! Let the Joy-bells ring!
Ring out all doubt and fear.
Ring in the good of brotherhood,
Throughout the coming year.

The Swimmin' Hole

by Pearl Howerton

Let the years roll backward one by one
To happy days when I was young,
Back to the boyhood days of old
And the friends I met at the swimmin' hole.

The world was ours in the bygone days
As we went our happy, carefree ways.
No bitterness or greed had touched our soul
When we were boys at the swimmin' hole.

We dreamed of the future far and dim—
Things we'd do when we were men,
With never a thought of growing old
When we were boys at the swimmin' hole.

Bill, a hunter brave would be
And ride the prairie, wild and free.
He talked of buffalo and shaggy furs,
Swift-footed horses, and silver spurs.

Young Ned would sail the seven seas
With silver buckles at his knees.
Bold adventures were his goal
When we planned our lives at the swimmin' hole.

Me? I had no yen to roam;
I was content to stay at home.
My country called for me one day
Then like the others I sailed away.

Three years I gave to Uncle Sam—
I left a leg in No Man's Land.
They sent me home, my duty done,
Life was finished before it'd begun.

Forty years have passed, and many more.
I sit beside my cottage door
And dream of happy days of old
And the friends I met at the swimmin' hole.

My eyes grow dim as the years roll on;
Most of my friends have long been gone.
Time and wars have taken their toll
Of the boys who met at the swimmin' hole.

The Tax Age

by Pearl Howerton

We have had the stone age, the cave man age and old age,
We've had the roaring teen age; and now we've got the tax age.
And if you are not aging, brother, I'm sure that you soon will,
When you realize what has happened to our little dollar bill.

There was a time when this small dollar would buy a lot of things,
Thread and buttons for my dress, also curlers for my bangs,
But that was in the long ago, before the world went wild,
And put a tax on everything, your house, your cow, your child.

And if you have a rooster to wake you in the morn,
They'll put a tax upon his head as sure as you are born,
They tax you for the air you breathe, the water that you drink,
For your aging Frigidaire, and your leaky kitchen sink.

I tell you what, this tax-mad age has really got me down,
Sometimes I think I'll bless the day they lay me in the ground,
When and if I get to Heaven, how happy I will be,
To find just one small corner with a sign that says, "Tax Free."

Thanksgiving at Grandma's

by Pearl Howerton
(1st version)

A second version was published in the *Prospect News* and a local magazine; however, this version is more complete.

We always go to Grandma's
  On Thanksgiving Day,
There we meet our kith and kin
  From many miles away.

They come with well filled baskets,
  These uncles, aunts, and cousins,
With pumpkin pie and gingerbread, and
  Cookies by the dozens.

Grandma's house is big and warm
  There's lots of room to play,
It's always fun at grandma's house
  On Thanksgiving Day.

The turkey's roasted to a turn,
  The ham is golden brown,
With gravy sizzling in the pan
  And potatoes all around.

With this food spread all about
  It is so hard to wait
When it's dinner time at Grandma's
  And a boy is only eight.

At last the food is on the table
  With Everyone in place,
Then I hear my grandma say,
  "Father, will you say the grace?"

My grandpa bows a humble head
  And then begins to pray,
His prayers are always longer
  On Thanksgiving Day.

He asked the Lord to bless our food
  And on our distant kin,
Who had come from far away
  To share this day with him.

He asked the Lord to guard our boys
  Who sailed across the sea
To fight our country's battles
  To keep our homeland free.

I once saw Aunt Samantha
  Wipe a teardrop from her eye,
I was sure that it would fall
  Right in the pumpkin pie.

Grandpa stopped to catch a breath,
  And before he could start again,
I looked at all that tempting food
  And said a loud AMEN!

That Little Girl of Mine

by Pearl Howerton
to Pat on her birthday (June 29, 1973)

She was a tiny, lovely sprite:
That little girl of mine—
Soft brown ringlets on her neck
And two brown eyes that'd shine.

She was soft and lovely as a rose
With a smile that was divine.
And I loved her very much
That little girl of mine.

She had a great imagination
That little girl of mine.
Some days she was a cowboy
Who kept her boots and saddle
  shined.

She liked to play cops and robbers
Chasing outlaws was her line.
She always brought the bad guys
  down
That little girl of mine.

She even put on boxing gloves
At the tender age of nine,
Smashed the nose of my neighbor's
  son
That little girl of mine.

She grew into a lovely maiden
Leaving those childish games behind.
Lovers came from far and near
To worship at her shrine.

If I could just rewind the years,
And live them one more time
And once again tuck into bed
That little girl of mine.

She now has children of her own
And a husband true and kind.
But to me she will always be
That little girl of mine.

Tiny Tim

by Pearl Howerton
(July 1970)

I was born an ugly little baby
Way down in my Ozark home.
My daddy looked at me and said,
"Something has gone wrong."

"This is not the son I wanted
To carry on my name,
To take his place in the field of sports,
And win renown and fame."

I was sure a disappointment
To my mom and dad.
They thought of how I'd let them down;
It made me very sad.

I grew into an ugly kid
With freckles and red hair.
It was very plain to see
I had no brains to spare.

My legs were bowed; I had buck teeth;
My shoulders, they were thin.
At school the kids all laughed at me
And called me Tiny Tim.

Chorus
Tiny Tim, Tiny Tim,
They called me Tiny Tim.
At school the kids all laughed at me
And called me Tiny Tim.

The Thrifty Shopper

by Pearl Howerton
(January 1975)

I have a little friend
Who grocery shops for me.
How she manipulates the grocer
Is something else to see.

I know the food prices of today
Give her a terrible shock;
And when they spring a new one
Her knees begin to knock.

But like the soldier that she is
She wades right into battle.
Sometimes she has money left
But never enough to rattle

She squeezes the tomatoes
To see if they are fresh.
The grocer gets so nervous
He breaks out with a rash.

He dares not offer her
A chicken thin and scrawny.
She takes one look and says,
"This jest ain't worth the money!"

Leisurely, she walks the store
Turning things round and round.
She must find just what she wants
Before she lays her money down.

She shakes this and pokes at that
Undecided what to choose,
While the poor harassed grocer
Is shaking in his shoes.

He often frowns and glares,
There's no use trying to stop her.
"No sir, you don't fool around
With this thrifty little shopper."

You ask me who the shopper is.
Her name I will not tell.
But for her shrewdness and ability
I'm sure you know her well.

To Bruce and Gayle – For Your Wedding

by Pearl Howerton
(April 1975)

Today the wedding bells are ringing
For these dear grandchildren of mine.
Now they start their lifelong journey
Down the misty years of time.

They're starting life in a bright, new
  world
That they may conquer if God wills.
May it never disappoint them
But all their dreams fulfill.

This highway of life on which they
  travel
Unfolding at their feet
May have thorns among the roses
And some bitter with the sweet.

But this they will overcome
As did the knights of old,
But press ever onward and upward
To reach their cherished goal.

They are brave and gallant soldiers
Marching down the years of time;
May they keep in step with truth and
  honor
And always keep their armor shined.

Together they will fight the storms of life
When hope is almost gone.
But their love for each other
Will give them courage to press on.

On this broad highway of life,
May their love grow stronger with the
  years.
Let them bypass all the heartaches
And gather roses instead of tears.

May the gracious God watch over them
These dear ones of mine,
And shower His blessings on them
Right down to the end of time.

To Cathy

by Pearl Howerton
for her granddaughter Cathy Howerton (July 23, 1972)

I know a lovely, little girl
Who sometimes calls me Gran.
Round her throat she often wears
A soft, blue velvet band.

She is gentle, kind, and sweet
And wears a diamond on her hand.
One day soon she'll be a bride,
This little girl in the blue velvet band.

She is in love with a wonderful man
This girl who calls me Gran.
She'll walk with him down life's long highway
This little girl in the blue velvet band.

Her hair is as soft as the wing of a dove,
Her eyes are blue as the heavens grand,
Her smile is like the morning sun,
This little girl in the blue velvet band.

May her footsteps never walk
The path of shifting sands
But ever walk in the narrow way—
This little girl in the blue velvet band.

I wish life's best for this little girl
Who sometimes calls me Gran.
And may she find her pot of gold
This little girl in the blue velvet band.

To Cindy

by Pearl Howerton
for Cindy Jones (1974)

The happy school days are over
For this little friend of mine.
Now she starts her lifelong journey
Down the misty years of time.

She's starting life in a bright, new world
That she may conquer if God wills.
May it never disappoint her
But all her dreams fulfill.

This highway of life on which she stands
Unfolding at her feet,
May have thorns among the roses
And some bitter with the sweet.

But this she will overcome
This little girls with heart of gold.
But she will press ever onward
To reach her cherished goal.

She is a blessing to her parents
This little maid so fair
Whom the gracious God so kindly
Has placed within their care.

I was a guest in her home
One lovely Christmas day.
With her grace and gentle kindness
She came into my heart to stay.

She is lovely as an April dawn
This little girl so fair
With eyes that sparkle like the dew
And star dust in her hair.

May her path be strewn with roses
Down through the passing years.
And may she never, never feel
The thorns of doubt and fear.

May the gracious God watch over her,
This little friend of mine,
And let her dance on a golden rainbow
Right down to the end of times.

To Frank and Debbie

by Pearl Howerton
to Debbie Koogle for her wedding

Franklin met the lovely Debbie
In nineteen hundred and seventy-one
And from this casual meeting
A lasting friendship sprung.

This friendship blossomed into love;
Love they had never known before.
And they became engaged
In nineteen hundred and seventy-four.

In June nineteen seventy-five
The wedding bells will chime.
They will start their lifelong journey
Down the years of time.

They're entering into a bright, new world
That they may conquer if God wills.
May it never disappoint them
But all their dreams fulfill.

This highway of life on which they travel
Unfolding at their feet
May have thorns among the roses
And some bitter with the sweet.

But this they will overcome,
These lovers brave and bold
And press ever onward
To reach their cherished goal.

Together they will fight the storms of life
When hope is almost gone.
But their love for each other
Will give them courage to press on.

On this broad highway of life
May their love grow stronger with the years;
Let them bypass all the heartaches
And reap happiness instead of tears.

May the gracious God watch over them
And guide them all the way;
And may their love grow stronger
With each passing golden day.

To Linda

by Pearl Howerton
(September 2, 1973)

I have a special friend
Who is very kind to me.
She writes and reads my letters,
For I can hardly see.

She often comes to visit me
And when my skies are gray,
Her sunny smile and helping hands
Soon drive the clouds away.

Our generation gap is very wide
For I am her great aunt you see.
And the hours we spend together
Are very dear to me.

I tell her tales of long ago
When the West was young,
How her great grandfather rode the range,
And saw a rustler hung.

She listens rapt and wide-eyed
To these stories of the past—
When her ancestors lived in sod shanties
Made from dobie mud and grass.

This is the wish of her great aunt
Who is writing this little rhyme:
May happiness and joy be with her
Right down to the end of time.

May the gracious God watch over her;
Let all her clouds be silver-lined;
And keep a rainbow in the skies
For this very dear friend of mine.

To Loren on His Birthday

by Pearl Howerton
for her son, Loren Howerton (August 24, 1973)

On the day of our Lord
Nineteen hundred and twenty-eight,
On a hot and sultry August day
The stork was running late.

We heard a tapping at the door
And the stork was standing there;
He was travel-stained and weary
With a look of deep despair.

He said, "I've traveled many miles
To bring this baby boy to you.
He fought and kicked me all the way;
You can see I'm black and blue.

We bade the stork to come in
And took you from his pouch.
I do believe you pinched him
For he loudly hollered, "OUCH!"

He said, "I'll sit and rest a spell
And watch the other storks go by,
And then I think I'll walk a while;
I am too pooped to fly."

The last I saw of the poor old stork
He was wobbling down the road.
His wings were drooping and his tail was dragging
From carrying such a heavy load.

To Tami Leigh on Her First Birthday

by Grandma Pearl Howerton
(September 11, 1972)

One bright and sunny autumn day
A treasure came to me:
A laughing blue-eyed, baby girl;
We called her Tami Leigh.

I'm sure the angels sent her
Straight down from Heaven above
To fill our home with sunshine
And to fill our hearts with love.

She is like a golden sunbeam,
Dancing everywhere—
Beneath the table with her doll
And sliding down the stairs.

Sometimes she is an angel
With laughter in her eyes;
Sometimes she is a little imp
That fills us with surprise.

Imp or angel, good or bad,
We love this little sprite,
Who truly is an angel
Shen she says her prayers at night.

We thank you God for this small treasure
You placed within our care;
And may we ever be found worthy,
Her precious life to share.

To Tonia Sue

by Pearl Howerton
to her granddaughter, Tonia Sue Gibson (1954)

I have a little friend;
Her name is Tonia Sue.
She flits and sings about the house
The whole day through.

She helps her Mama in the house,
Her Daddy on the lawn,
And keeps her baby brother quiet
When the television's on.

Her hair is brown;
Her eyes are green;
Her freckles are but few;
Her face is like the buttercups
When kissed by morning dew.

I tell you what this little Sue
Is really on the ball;
When it comes to helper-outers
She can't be beat at all.

She goes to church and Sunday school
And learns her lessons well.
In quoting jokes and riddles,
She really rings the bell.

You wonder why this little miss
Should mean so much to me?
Here is the little secret,
I'm her Grandma, don't you see?

To Willow

by Grandma Pearl Howerton
For Willow-eze at Christmas (1967)

I have a little grandchild,
I call her Willow-eze.
She plays and flits about the house
Like a lovely summer breeze.

Her eyes are blue as violets
Touched by the morning dew,
Her hair is soft and silky
With sunbeams breaking through.

She likes to help her old Grandma,
In every way she can;
While helping me make dinner,
She upset my frying pan.

She quickly ran to fetch the mop
This little maid so neat,
She gave one swipe across the floor
And swept me off my feet!

She then ran calling to the door,
For Tom-Tom and Cindy-Lou
When they heard their little miss,
They knew just what to do.

They scurried through the kitchen
  door
And viewed with great surprise,
My pan of tasty gravy
Lying there before their eyes.

They licked and slurped and growled
  a bit
Then licked and slurped some more.
Soon there was no gravy left,
On the shiny kitchen floor.

But there was Grandma, sad to say,
Flat against the kitchen wall.
I was shaken up and groggy,
For great had been my fall!

"Now, Grandma, don't you worry,"
She said to me so sweet.
"If you will only help a bit,
We'll get you on your feet."

She then reached down two little
  hands
And gave a mighty yank,
I slid across that shiny floor
Right up against the sink.

I tell you this, my little maid,
Always sees her troubles through
With the timely help of Tom-Tom
And her faithful Cindy-Lou.

The Vagabond Lover

by Pearl Howerton
for Bruce and Gayle (June 1973)

I'm just a vagabond lover
With a pocket full of dreams;
I'm searching for a vagabond sweetheart
To share with me those dreams.

I have no gold to offer,
But the wealth of the world is mine:
The mountain peaks and desert sands
And my guiding star that shines.

If I find a sweetheart
Who will wander by my side,
We'll roam the world together,
Me and my vagabond bride.

We'll share the beauties of the world
That God has given to man,
Me and my little vagabond bride
As we wander hand in hand.

We'll roam free as the south winds
That roll across the summer sky,
One with God and nature
My vagabond bride and I.

We'll climb to the highest mountain top
Where the eagle builds her nest.
We'll wander through the valleys
When the sun sinks low in the west.

We'll roam to strange and distant places
Down highways wide and long.
We'll sit by our campfires eventides
And sing our vagabond song.

The Village Grocer

by Pearl Howerton
for her son Loren on this birthday (1972)

My son is the village grocer;
His troubles they are many
When the small fry come to town
With their nickels, dimes, and pennies.

One by one and two by two
They beat a path right to his door.
To them, the nearest thing to heaven
Is the village grocery store.

The little boy with his "viniger" bottle
Who always came at night;
"Please sir, I can't say it,
But smell this bottle and give me a
pint."

Mrs. Jones rushed in one day
Very hot and riled.
She yelled, "That milk you sold me
Has done gone and sp'iled."

The poor, tired grocer bravely smiled
And gave her another bottle.
And as she left the store, he said,
"There's a neck I'd like to throttle."

The timid, little Mrs. Gray
Who is very kind and sweet
Comes in almost every day
For something her poor husband can
eat.

Her husband is very poorly
And sometimes hard to please.
Today he thinks he'd like to have
Some beer and Limburger cheese.

Then comes in the heavy spender:
She wants a loaf of bread, pound of
coffee,
And a quarter's worth of beans,
And a small piece of hog jowl to
"b'ile" in her turnip greens.

Then there are the squeezers and
pinchers.
They squeeze the Charmin, lettuce,
and tomatoes.
They squeeze and pinch everything
in sight
Then buy three pounds of potatoes.

Then there comes the day
When nothing seems to go right.
He prays, "Lord, help me through
this day,
I'll try to make it through the night."

The Village Tattlers

by Pearl Howerton

The tattlers are a busy people.
They go from door to door
Leaving juicy bits of gossip
And picking up a little more.

They do not seem to realize,
Nor little do they care,
How many homes were saddened
By their visits there.

A tale that starts in idle gossip
May grow in leaps and bounds
Until some poor and innocent soul
Becomes the outcast of the town.

Tattlers go to church on Sunday,
Sing in the village choir,
And try to let the people see
Just how good they really are.

They ask you, "Have you heard the
  news
That's going around the town?"
They say that no-good Mr. X
Has been seeing Mrs. Brown.

They think her husband should be
  told
And they know him very well;
But as they do not carry tales
They're not the ones to tell.

But Mr. Brown ***was*** told one day
And his home was broken up.
Score another point for the tattlers—
For the lives that they disrupt.

Here are some true and timely
  words—
Words that a wise man wrote;
They may help us very much
When we're tempted—and I quote:

"There is so much good in the worst
  of us,
And so much bad in the best of us,
That it ill behooves any of us
To talk about the rest of us."

The Waiting Room

by Pearl Howerton
(June 1968)

I have a lovely waiting room
In a home for the feeble and old,
And though its warm and sunny,
I seem to shiver with cold.

The floors are smooth and polished
The walls are soft and nice,
They seem to close about me
Like arms of chilling ice.

My waiting room is lovely
It's always clean and neat,
A rocking chair in the corner
A bed with fresh white sheets.

I sit in my lovely waiting room
And dream of the by-gone years
When I held my children on my
knee
And dried their baby tears.

I feign would hold them to my heart
As in those days of yore,
And sooth their childish fears away
As oft I've done before.

They've grown to men and women
now
And left us, one by one,
To try their wings in other lands
And find their places in the sun.

John and I are now alone
Where we came as bride and groom.
We seem to hear their childish voices
Echoing from room to room.

We were happy, John and I
We had many golden years;
Then one day I was left alone
Burdened with grief and fears.

All alone, too tired to care
Nor with the will to carry on,
Then one day, I found myself
In this lovely Old Folks Home.

I am resigned to my waiting room
As those about me are.
I hope for a place in heaven
When I'm called to cross the bar.

The Weary Pilgrim

by Pearl Howerton

I'm just a weary pilgrim, on this broad highway of life.
In search of that great city, where comes no toil or strife,
I've traveled this wide world over; over hill and plains I roam.
I'm just a weary pilgrim, I'm searching for a home.

I'm just a weary pilgrim; I'm sad; I'm weak; I'm lorn.
But Christ the Lord has promised me a beautiful heavenly home.
My trials will soon be over; no longer will I roam.
I'm just a weary pilgrim; I'm on my journey home.

I'm just a weary pilgrim; I'm weak and tempest-tossed.
I'll rest upon His promise, and I shall not be lost.
He says that whosoever will, to him may freely come;
I'm just a weary pilgrim; I'm on my journey home.

Wedding Bells

by Pearl Howerton
for Cathy and Tom (May 26, 1973)

Today the wedding bells are ringing
For this dear grandchild of mine.
And though I'm many miles away,
I can almost hear them chime.

With the lover of her choice
She stands on the threshold of life,
To faithfully walk beside him
A true and loyal wife.

Her heart aglow with hope and love,
On this her wedding day—
Hope that her happiness and love
Will never slip away.

May the golden bells of joy ring out
For her down through the years.
And may she never feel
The thorns of doubt and fear.

May the gracious God watch over her
And guide her footsteps right
And shower His greatest blessings
On this little girl in white.

Give her strength and wisdom,
On entering this highway of life,
To be a faithful helpmate
And an understanding wife.

May she always walk in the sunlight
And all her clouds be silvery lined
With always a beautiful rainbow.
For this dear grandchild of mine.

What Will the Neighbors Say?

by Pearl Howerton

All my life I've been a slave,
To this cowardly little phrase,
That ruled my every waking thought,
"What will the neighbors say?"

I'd like to do some crazy thing,
When I greet each newborn day,
Open my windows, shout and sing,
But what would the neighbors say?

I'd like to run and shout,
With the kids across the way,
Turn some cartwheels and somersaults,
But what would the neighbors say?

I'd like to walk in the summer rain,
And feel its cooling spray,
Then wade barefoot in the mud,
But what would the neighbors say?

I'd like to help some poor soul,
Who has stumbled on life's way,
A helping hand, and a few kind words,
But what would the neighbors say?

The sins of omission are many,
So the scriptures say.
I have sinned ten-thousand-fold,
Forgive me Lord I pray.

What will the neighbors say?
Has haunted my whole life through,
But when it's time to pay,
What can the neighbors do?

When my sojourn here is ended,
And I face the Judgement Day,
When I knock at the Pearly Gates,
What will St. Peter say?

When Grandma Was a Girl

by Pearl Howerton
(October 1968)

When my Grandma was a girl,
Back in the long ago,
She danced the light fandango,
And the Spanish heel and toe.

She tripped and swirled about the floor
As light as thistle down.
She was the envy of her friends
And the beauty of the town.

Her skirts were wide and ruffled,
Her hair was black as jet,
She had ribbon, lace, and frills
On her little panti-lets.

Her little shoes were pointed;
Her bustle set just right;
Her waist was slim and dainty
Cause it was laced so tight.

When she tripped along the street
With her little parasol,
I'm sure the warm spring sunshine
Didn't touch her face at all.

Her eyes were dark as midnight;
On her cheeks there was a glow.
How do I know all this?
Why my Grandma told me so.

I'm sure that in the long ago
No sweeter maid could be found.
But something happened to my Grandma,
'Cause she weighs two hundred pounds.

When the Rain Came Down

by Pearl Howerton

I remember that hot, dry summer,
When the sun like shining brass,
Dried the rivers and the lakes,
And parched the meadow grass.

The thermometer stood at a hundred and four
For many long hot days.
The earth was like a furnace
From the sun's hot blistering rays.

Heat devils danced across the fields
That once were lush and green,
In the stillness of this heat
Not a moving twig could be seen.

Cattle stood in the dry creek bed
Where once cool water flowed,
With lowered heads and parched tongues
The sniffed the drying mud.

Farmers watched the brassy skies,
And prayed for precious rain
To cool the parched and drying earth,
And save their fields of grain.

Heat like an omen of doom
Hung over the country and town
The heavens seemed to open,
And then the rain came down.

The precious cool, life-giving rain
Restored the fields so parched and brown
Folks bowed their heads and humbly prayed
When at last the rain came down.

A White Winter Day

by Pearl Howerton
(October 1970)

Aboard a northbound train
For a long and lonely ride,
We left the crowded, smoky city
For the open countryside.

Snow had fallen in the night
Covering field and hill.
In the quiet of that early dawn,
The whole world was standing still.

Each house was a magic castle—
The roofs with snow piled high.
While from the many chimney pots
Smoke slowly drifted to the sky.

The sky was like a huge white bowl
Enclosing a world of snow and ice
That glistens in the morning sun
Like the gates of paradise.

Artists have often tried to paint
Scenes and places such as this;
But in their greatest efforts
There's something they have missed.

They missed the beauty of the rising sun
That sets this world aglow,
Candles lit in the treetops,
And diamonds sprinkled in the snow.

Gems of many colors
Shone from bush and trees
And flowed beside our speeding train
Like waves on a crystal sea.

My trip that started out so drab
Had truly turned to bliss.
I think that I shall never again
See beauty such as this.

Wide River

by Pearl Howerton

Roll on wide river on your way to the sea;
Won't you please whisper a song to me?
Of beautiful places that you have seen
Rolling hills and meadows green.

Flow softly wide river as you roll along
That I may grasp the theme of your song;
Sing of mountains and drifting sands
Of sunny beaches and far-away lands.

Roll on wide river; roll on to the sea.
Tell me of friends who are dear to me,
Who have drifted away like your flowing tide
Down to the ocean so deep and wide.

Roll on wide river; roll on
Forever singing an endless song.
Let me drift with your tide that laps the shore,
Till life and time shall be no more.

The Wind

by Pearl Howerton

You cannot see the wind
Though it is always nigh,
In the stillness of the night
You hear it breath and sigh.

It moans about the chimney pots
Around the window sill,
And sings a soft, low lullaby
When all the world is still.

It soothes the weary traveler
With sweat upon his brow,
And whispers music in the trees
Up to the topmost bough.

The wind is soft and gentle
In the balmy summer time,
But when the gods are angry
It becomes a roaring lion.

It whips the ocean into waves
That beat upon the shore,
And leaves destruction in its wake
Till it has ceased to roar.

The wind is also helpful
I'm sure you will agree,
It sailed our Pilgrim Fathers
From a land beyond the sea.

It sails the clouds like pirate ships
Across the summer sky,
When the daisies bow and nod
The wind is passing by.

You cannot see the wind
Though it is always near,
It brings us soothing comfort
As well as darkest fear.

Winter

by Pearl Howerton

Winter comes with a driving blast;
Blanketing snow falls thick and fast,
Hiding every grassy plot,
Covering roof and chimney pot.

The cold winds blow and snowflakes fall
On the walks and garden walls.
On the meadows once so green,
Not a blade or twig is seen.

The brown hills wear an ermine cloak;
Snowy plumes adorn the oak;
A crown of snowflakes the pine tree wears
Like jewels in a maiden's hair.

In this winter wonderland,
Children shout with glee;
Their bobsleds race right down the hill,
Voices ringing loud and free.

The cold wind blows and nips the toes,
Paints cherry-red each little nose,
Numbs the hands that guide the sleigh
Down the hill at the close of day.

Wishes

by Pearl Howerton
(January 29, 1970)

I know that wishes are seldom granted
Yet I would ask a few—
To always be able to see
Fields and meadows drenched with dew.

I wish that wars would forever cease
And men both black and white
Could be united in brotherhood
And strive for what is right.

I would wish that never again
Would the world hear battle cries,
Where men for greed and power
Force our noble sons to die.

I wish that hungry children
At home and across the sea
Might have comfort, food, and shelter
In a world forever free.

I would wish that battlefields
Where brave men fight and die
Could again see crimson poppies
Lift their faces to the sky–

This is only wishful dreaming
And wishes seldom do come true;
But please dear Grantor of Wishes
Grant me just a few.

Bonnie in front of Mack and Pearl Howerton, 1951.

Pearl Reading a book in the orchard, circa 1955.

Grandmothers Pearl Howerton and Frona Braschler with Bonnie Gibson on her lap, August 1954 at Howerton's rock house on Y Highway.

Back row: Pearl, Maxine, Mack. Front row: Tonia, Keith, Bonnie, August 22 1956.

Pearl haloed by one of her smocked cushions.

Pearl in her fifties.

Pearl's 80th birthday

Mack Henry Howerton and Pearl Merriman Howerton, ca. 1957.

Maxine and Pearl, circa 1968

Pictured l-r: Mack and Pearl Howerton, Dorothy & Arthur Keeny, Tonia Gibson, Frona Braschler, Keith, Jack holding Randy & Bonnie Gibson, and Big Weaver Braschler.

Reflections on Grandma Pearl Howerton

from the Memoirs of Bonnie Lou Gibson Risby

My mother, Maxine Gibson, was the best cook that I ever met—and I've known a few. I mention this simply because she is the only cook superior to my two Grandmothers, Pearl Howerton and Frona Patterson Gibson Braschler.

Mom's mother, Pearl, could make the most incredible light rolls and homemade bread in seven counties. Even when she was legally blind and living in the little pink house on Jackson, people came to pick up their bread on baking day. I often helped her sift, mix, knead, punch down and divide dough into loaves. Pearl used leftover mashed potatoes to feed her yeast and could make bread as effortlessly as most people comb their hair. I would copy down amounts and methods even though Pearl never used a recipe. My rolls would never smell and taste as good as Grandma's. (Recipes later)

During my lifetime, most of Pearl's baking was done in a gas oven but she was also expert in regulating wood-burning ones—which is not as easy as it sounds. You could not just preheat to a standard temperature. You "chunked" in cord wood until you had an even heat and then cooled it to baking temperature by setting the oven door ajar.

Grandma Pearl could also fry the most delectable fish and frog legs and bake sumptuous cornbread. She enjoyed fresh fish and game as much as anyone I ever knew.

I should probably mention that most of my visits to Pearl's occurred during the summertime so I have endless memories of her blackberry and peach cobblers. If I was paid a million dollars to choose one of her cobblers as superior, I would just keep tasting until nothing was left and then announce, "whippoorwill or meadowlark" just too good to choose.

Summers "in the country" meant kettles of string beans, new potatoes the size of golf balls and marbles, saucer-sized tomato slices, okra, purple hull peas, corn on the cob, brined cucumber-onion salad, white beans with smoked jowl, spring onions, squash, and wilted lettuce. There were pies, cobblers and individual fried pies filled with peaches, plums or tart summer apples.

When I was almost sixteen, a friend brought Pearl a peck of Concorde grapes for jelly but she decided to make pies instead. I loved every variety of her pies but had never heard of grape pies. I helped Pearl squeeze each grape out of its skin, saving the skins in one pot and the "innards" in another. After the separation, she heated the insides on the stove, mashed them with a potato masher as they simmered and then sieved out all the seeds before returning the skins to the mixture. The delectably aromatic purple mass was sweetened and thickened just enough, cooled a bit, poured into pie shells, dotted with butter and sealed with top crusts into which large slits were cut to let out steam and a little of the tantalizing filling. These pies smelled so good during the baking that I knew I could never wait until after dinner. Pearl suggested that we have dessert first that evening–which I did. That was probably the best pie I ever ate.

Grandma was a traditional country cook but as she traveled she added new menus to her repertoire. She became quite a hand at chicken Chow Mein and almost always had the fixings in her pantry. There was nothing that Pearl would not attempt to cook (or sew or build). If someone ran a trotline, she fried fish; if someone brought her a mess of quail, she braised quail; squirrel, she made peppery dumplings in savory gravy; ducks, she made sage dressing; rabbits, she created fricassee. She was very imaginative and creative in the kitchen and her sewing room.

Grandma Pearl had more lyrics and yarns stored in her brain than most people have cataloged in their libraries. We pestered her mercilessly to perform for us on every visit. "Sing *Barb'ra Allen*. Sing *Gotta Stop Kickin' My Dog Around*. Sing *The Preacher and the Bear*. Sing *My Little Old Sod Shanty on the Claim*. Sing *Flow Gently Sweet Afton*." She lead us in ballads that made us cry or laugh. She never ran dry and we loved it.

We also loved Grandma Pearl's tales of early life on the Kansas Prairie. Pearl's mother was pregnant during the wagon train journey to Kansas; Pearl was born shortly after their arrival on June 14, 1888. I am not sure how many years they lived in Kansas before returning home to Missouri.

One of Pearl's daily chores as a very young child was gathering fuel. There were no trees providing kindling or cord wood. The family cooked and heated their home with buffalo chips which were abundant on the prairie. Pearl and Fred (her brother closest to her in age) wandered the prairie gathering dried chips. Green chips were flipped over with a stick allowing them to cure under the prairie sun so they could be collected later. Pearl vouched that chips were good fuel. They burned hot and steady and surprisingly without any odor other than burning grass. Nancy Ann Hardesty Merriman never minded cooking the family's meals over them except when the circuit-rider came for dinner. Then she was a bit embarrassed as Pearl recalled.

Nancy Ann's forlorn parents pined for their once-pampered only child struggling with the hardships of frontier life. They sent her a train ticket once a year so she could come "home" for a visit. The Merriman children, except for the youngest baby, were left behind on the prairie while their mother returned east. Pearl remembers these periods of her mother's absences to be among the most arduous.

Pearl, the oldest girl, was put in charge of cooking for a large group of men even though she was too short to reach the stove. She had to stand on a chair to prepare large meals. She was also expected to do laundry and a host of chores. But Pearl was not unlike other frontier girls and never complained about what was expected. It was unthinkable not to shoulder your load.

Upon arriving in Kansas, the family weathered the first bitter winter in a combination dugout-sod shanty.

A dugout was a prairie home built into the side of a slope so that only one wall and a roof were required. Many families "dug in" for winter using their wagon canvas as a lining for their roof. A dugout was quick and cheap and kept a family snug, if not comfortable, until they could work their claim and establish roots.

A sod shanty was a structure built from blocks of sod cut from the prairie's immense resource of grass. The grass blocks were stacked in the fashion of bricks. The sod quickly rooted itself together so blocks needed no mortar. The walls actually bloomed in springtime. A shanty could withstand the harsh realities of life on the prairie. Many families spent years in sod shanties.

But Orlando Llewellyn Merriman was a good carpenter and determined to build a proper frame home from lumber which was delivered to the railhead near present-day Kingman City, Kansas. This was only a generation or so after the Civil War. Following that war, Kansas was a huge player in westward expansion. 1860 marked the first locomotive in Kansas. By 1874 four railroads shipped over 122,900 head of Texas cattle to Kansas in eight months. The Kansas Pacific merged with the Union Pacific and the population of Kansas increased from one hundred thousand to well over a million. Trail herds headed for Dodge City, Wichita, and Topeka. Kansas was booming and Orlando's carpentry skills were in high demand.

I should mention that the bulk of all the crossties used for rail expansion into the western states were hewn from white oaks from the Missouri Ozarks. This expansion led to earning Doniphan its one-time title of Tie Capital of the World. Orlando and his sons would soon return home joining the leagues of men hand hewing logs into ties.

On the prairie, the Merriman family retained not only the wagon they arrived in but also their team of oxen. In addition to their standard 160-acre homestead, they were awarded additional land as a *tree-stead*. Nancy's parents continuously shipped saplings to Kansas which were carefully planted, nurtured and routinely died. All lumber necessary for Orlando's carpentry was shipped from the east.

The family gardened, hunted and fed itself from the prairie. Even soap came from the prairie's yucca plants. But coffee, sugar, cloth, and other staples as well as lumber, nails and tools had to be purchased. Also, grain harvested must go to the railhead to be sold. So trips to the railhead were necessary.

I emphasize trips to the railhead primarily because these trips provide the backdrop for many of my favorite tales. Pearl had several brothers that were nearly a generation older than her.

One oft-told adventure belongs to one of these older brothers. In *Give Them Their Heads* I have attempted to retell Pearl's account.

Give Them Their Heads

It was a beautiful, blue-sky day in early spring when the lad started out, his heart singing with the freedom of abandoning chores for a foray across the burgeoning prairie. There was no reason for concern; he knew his way across the treeless plain having driven the docile team to town many times. It would be an all-day endeavor of blissful freedom. After a pre-dawn breakfast, Nancy tied two leftover biscuits and a baked sweet potato into a napkin for her son's lunch. He set off at once.

By midmorning, he arrived safely at the railhead and took care of business. He retrieved the family's precious mail from loved ones back east, filled his mother's bill of supplies at the mercantile, fetched his father's lumber order from the rail yard and loaded the wagon for the return trip. All this he accomplished well before midday. In no hurry to begin his return to the homestead, the boy enjoyed tarrying to exchange good humor and gossip with friends at the depot. His gab was cut short when a veteran of the prairie advised him, "better get a move on, Merriman. That western sky spells trouble."

The lad read nothing in the azure firmament but heeded the old-timer's advice. He was a third of the way home before the first snowflakes drifted down like white feathers. Soon the afternoon's sun was curtained leaving a counterfeit twilight. Within thirty minutes the traveler was enveloped in a full-force prairie blizzard. Whiteout conditions, brutal winds, and bone-chilling cold replaced the false spring of that morning. The pilgrim knew he had another four hours before reaching the warmth of home. Drifts of snow quickly cloaked the prairie's familiar landmarks.

Soon it was almost dark; his benchmarks were blurred by drifts. An hour after leaving town, our wayfarer was hopelessly lost. He knew the perils of being adrift on the frozen prairie. If forced to spend the night unsheltered, he was doomed. His frozen corpse would be found when the snow began to melt.

After surrendering to the severity of his predicament, our youth made a crucial decision. He would put his faith in God and the wisdom of old-timers he trusted.

"Give the oxen their head," they had often admonished. "Blizzards, dust storms, prairie fires. Just give the oxen their head." Without options, he dropped the reins and scrambled down from the wagon seat. He waited beside the wagon.

Jake and Zeke stood still a long time waiting for his "walk on" command. The boy pulled up his collar and wedged his hat far down on his brow while hunching his shoulders against the brutal gale. Gradually, the animals realized no command was coming and began to move on their own accord. They put their heads low to the ground and plodded into the wind. Occasionally they would bawl but their pitiful lows were drowned out by the howls of the Kansas tempest.

Our wanderer would have frozen sitting in the wagon. Trudging kept him warm while insulating his mind against the dread of being lost. Young Merriman never let go of the wagon's leather straps for fear of being cast adrift without a lifeline. Stumbling his way through drifts, his feet became heavy and numb but the youth kept his nerve and followed his sturdy team for what seemed like days. Finally the wind died down and eerie silence replaced its wintery plaint. Even without the tumult, snow continued to powder down and the teen's extremities were numb.

There were no stars or moon to reflect on the sea of white, just an uncanny glow that gave the scene a dreamlike quality. The lad trudged on having no idea of his bearings or whether the oxen led him toward home or further from it. After trekking many hours, he thought he saw a distant star low on the horizon. "Was the storm lifting?" he wondered.

Maybe his frozen body had begun to play tricks on his mind. Mirage or omen, the star was a welcome distraction. The exhausted boy knew he must walk on or die. Repose in the wagon was out of the question. Rest would bring sleep and sleep would bring death. He trudged on with frozen, rag-wrapped fingers clinging to the wagon strap. Survival solely depended on the homing instincts of Jake and Zeke. He pinned his trust on his humble oxen and in his God which guided them.

Once again he thought he spied a star above the horizon but it vanished as the castaway wandered. Time and again the tiny star appeared only to vanish. Maybe it was his imagination but the team seemed to be moving toward it.

"Yes," he convinced himself, "they really are moving toward that tiny star just as the caravan of the Magi moved toward that other star so long ago." A glimmer of hope sprang within his chest as the magnitude of the star seemed to grow. But the sky overhead remained blanketed by clouds—no stars could be visible. "What star hangs so close to the horizon?" His pondering was interrupted by the wind calling out his name. Not a howl as it had been earlier, but a siren's voice flowing into his ears. He listened intently. But all that came to his straining ears was the crunching of snow under his frozen boots and the steady breathing of his oxen. His ears strained against the disappointing silence.

Minutes later, the wind again shouted his name. His heart leapt up. He answered the wind with all his might, "I'm here! I'm here!"

But there was no answer. "Am I losing my mind?" he wondered.

Once again the wind again shouted his name.

Crazy or not he answered.

His cry was echoed by a far-off acknowledgement. This time he recognized his name not in the language of the wind but in his own father's voice.

His rejoicing salutation echoed, "Hallooooooooo. I'm here! I'm here!"

Soon the oxen were rewarded with feed and shelter from the storm as the boy thawed in the cozy shanty embraced by his worried parents and siblings. There was no end to their making over the half-frozen lad. The faithful oxen had indeed found their way home guided by a compass beyond human comprehension.

By midday, Orlando Merriman had realized there was no way to find his homeward-bound son. Venturing onto the prairie in a blizzard would simply ensure disaster to prospective rescuers. In desperation, his father had lashed together his longest timbers erecting a makeshift tower to whose pinnacle he secured the family's strongest lanterns. He prayed that somehow their light would be a beacon through the blinding storm: a lighthouse on the prairie. His prayers and those of all the family were answered that night.

Pearl (center) with family, ca. 1950.

Recipes

Pearl's Hot Rolls and Sweet Rolls

(Bonnie wrote this down in 1970 while watching Grandma Pearl Howerton who never used a recipe but always had plenty of company on baking day.)

Hot Rolls

- Sprinkle 2 pkg. dry yeast onto a cup of warm water to proof.

  Add all together:
  ½ cup sugar
  1 tsp. salt
  ½ cup oil
  1 beaten egg *(optional)*
  ½ cup potato buds softened in about 1 cup warm water *(Before instant, Pearl used leftover mashed potatoes or a baked potato mashed with a fork. She also substituted potato water for part of her liquid. Her amounts varied.)*

- Next add yeast and 3 or 4 more cups warm water. Add enough flour until the dough can be handled. *(This takes a lot of flour.)*
- Knead on floured board until satiny. Place in greased bowl, cover with towel, and place in a warm area.
- Let dough rise *(double)*; punch down. Let rise again and punch down a second time.
- Cut dough into pieces and roll into balls for loaves or pinch off generous pieces for rolls. Rolls are rolled into balls *(golf ball size or a little larger)*. Place dough on greased trays to rest.
- Let rise *(almost double but not quite)*. Brush with melted butter or oil. Bake. Grandma did not give me a time or a temperature. I use a medium hot oven and a medium-sized loaf takes about 45 minutes. I let rolls touch on the sides so they will rise taller.

Notes: I brush the tops of loaves and rolls with butter right after they come out of the oven. The loaves will have a nice hollow sound if you thump on the crust with your finger. I serve this bread warm with unsalted sweet butter, fresh jam or preserves, molasses, or honey. It is a meal in itself.

Sweet Rolls

Grandma used pretty much the same recipe only doubling the sugar in the dough and adding freshly grated nutmeg *(to taste)*. The rising and punching was exactly the same.

Grandma told me to fashion this dough into any sweet roll that you desire with any filling that you desire.

I *(like my mother, Maxine)* roll out the dough *(into a long rectangle about ¼-inch-thick)*, butter generously, then sprinkle with cinnamon sugar with a little flour added to it; roll the generously sprinkled dough into logs, slice pinwheels *(1-inch thick)*, arrange them on baking trays, sprinkle tops with extra cinnamon sugar; let rise and bake in a medium hot oven (375 to 400).

Sometimes, I *(like my mother)* add raisins or chopped nuts on top of the cinnamon mixture before rolling into logs. I dunk the warm rolls in a glaze made of powdered sugar, milk, and vanilla or a glaze of powdered sugar and lemon juice *(add just enough liquid to give it a slightly runny consistency)*. If the baking pans have deeper sides, I just drizzle the glaze over, flooding the surface.

These moist rolls freeze wonderfully if you can keep any that long.

Bonnie's quick version of Grandma Howerton's Rolls

Pearl's light rolls and bread were legendary in Ripley County. On baking day, people stopped for a pan of rolls or a loaf of bread. Pearl never used a recipe but always offered her method to anyone interested. I have watched her making bread hundreds of times. In later years, Pearl added potato buds rather than mashed potatoes or potato water to her bread. Pearl's bread took most of the day. Below is my shortcut version that you can make in the time you cook a big dinner. It is "almost" as good Pearl's.

- Preheat oven to 400
- Scald 1 cup of milk, cool to lukewarm then sprinkle on one packet of dry yeast. Let set at least 5 minutes to bloom.

Meanwhile in a bowl, mix:

2 tablespoons of oil or melted butter
4 tablespoons sugar
1 egg (Pearl and Maxine added or omitted the egg, optional)
1 cup leftover mashed potatoes *(or baked potato mashed up)*
1-½ teaspoons salt *(If potatoes are salted adjust amount. Salt inhibits yeast.)*

- Then add yeast/milk mixture and mix gently.
- Add 1-½ cups flour and mix.
- Add additional 1-½ cups flour and mix. *(Add more or less depending on weather and flour type)*. Dough will be elastic and cling together but should be a little sticky at this point.
- Knead dough on floured surface until smooth and supple about 1 or 2 minutes. Dough will feel like a baby's bottom. Do not over work dough.
- For rolls, cut dough into 16 even portions and roll each into a ball.
- Place on a non-stick backing tray. Dunk each roll into melted butter and reposition on tray. *(Or you can brush tops with butter after they rise and again after they bake.)*
- Cover rolls with plastic wrap or dish towel, place in warm, draft-free location and allow rolls to double in size *(about 15 minutes)*. You can position rolls close so that the sides touch or not depending on whether you like more or less crust. Also rolls will rise higher when touching. *(If you need to slow down or hold, simply set the tray in the frig while you finish preparing your meal.)*
- Bake 12 to 15 minutes in center oven until tops are golden brown and the rolls sound hollow when tapped with your finger. Check the color of the bottoms to make sure rolls are done through.

Serve warm with lots of butter.

Maxine, Mack, Tonia, and Pearl, ca. 1946.

Bonnie, Tonia, Pearl, Mack, and Maxine (holding Keith), August 22, 1958.

Bonnie Lou Gibson Risby

Bonnie Risby grew up on several acres of Illinois woodland atop the bluffs across the Mississippi from St. Louis. These woods were her playground where she and her siblings camped out, played detective, scouted animals, hunted morels, learned to shoot, gardened and enjoyed the beauty of the outdoors in every season.

The Gibson's, a transplanted family following WWII, always felt they had a foot in two different states. With grandparents and extended family still living in Ripley County, Missouri, Bonnie and her family visited the Doniphan area several times a year spending holidays or school vacations and enjoying tubing, fishing, gigging, johnboat picnics, and family fish fries. Long before modern highways, these southbound journeys seemed much longer and each produced unique adventures involving detours, ice storms, carsickness, exasperated parents, and near-death car dilemmas.

After the birth of a new generation, pilgrimages to Ripley County continued although a bit modernized. Sons, daughters, nieces and nephews of the original transplants continued to wander back to Current River to visit family including many returning from afar after retirement.

Now third and fourth generations make an annual migration to their ancestral base to tend graves, visit relatives, frolic along the Current's crystal shoals creating new memories (despite sunburn and chigger bites), communing with the past and with nature.

Special Thanks

I want to thank the many people who have clipped newspapers and magazines to send Pearl's poems to me over the years. I know I may omit some very worthy folks; if you are one of them, you know who you are and I thank you. The following people have transcribed poems onto paper, typed, Xeroxed, clipped and tried to ensure a complete collection: Lillian Pepmiller, Geraldine Boyd Duncan, Maxine Howerton Gibson, Patricia Howerton Curran, Loren and Katie Howerton, Juanita Cermak, Margaret Dean, Naomi "Kitty" Braschler Burger, Wilma Holland, Helen Merriman Murdock, Lena McCauley, and Dottie Hunsaker. THANK YOU!

Index of Poems

Pearl Merriman Howerton, age 21 or 22.